THE ERECTION OF THE CROSS
And they crucified him, and parted his garments, casting lots . . .
(Matthew 27: 35)

THE
GOSPEL
ACCORDING TO
Shakefpeare:
The Pafsion

or

The Divine Tragœdy of
Jesus the Chrift
Part III

A Play in Verfe by
William Shakef-peare

Bafed on **The Holy Bible**
King James "Authorized" Verfion, 1611

The Pafsion of Our Lord and Saviour
Jesus the Chrift, fitted for the
pleafures and content of all Perfons
in Court, City, or Countrey.
The Greateft Story as it has never
been told before.

First Quarto

L O N D O N,

Printed for *R.D.Brown*, who authored allonymoufy
af *W. Shakspere* in name, to be folde by him, 2011

ALLONYMOUS BOOKS
A Division of Chi Xi Stigma Publishing Company, LLC
P.O. Box 3097
Pueblo, CO 81005

Website: www.chixistigma.org
Email: secretary@chixistigma.org

ISBN 13: 978-1-931608-30-5
ISBN 10: 1-931608-30-X

Dedicated to
John Michael Petric
My Constant Critic
Requiescat in pace

THE
GOSPEL
ACCORDING TO
Shakeſpeare:
The Paſsion

or

The Divine Tragedy of
Jeſus the Chriſt

Part III

DRAMATIS PERSONAE

JESUS & HIS DISCIPLES

Jesus, *the Christ*
Peter, *the Rock*
John, *the Beloved*
James, *the Greater*
James, *the Lesser*
Matthew, *the Publican*
Thomas, *the Doubter*
Bartholomew, *also known as Nathaniel*
Judas, *the Betrayer*

PHARISEES

Saul, *the Pharisee of Pharisees*
Nicodemus, *the Secret Disciple*
Caiaphas, *the High-Priest*
Malchus, *the Temple Guard*

THE ROMANS

Pontius Pilate, *the Prefect*
Herod Antipas, *the "King of the Jews", Roman collaborator*
The Centurian

THE WOMEN

Mary, Mother of Jesus
Mary Magdalene
Martha
Mary, Sister of Martha

THE WITNESSES

Witness to the Control of Nature
Witness to the Healing of the Leper
Witness to the Healing of the Blind
Witness to the Casting Out of Demons

Witness to the Resurrection of the Dead
A False Witness
A Second False Witness
A False Childhood Friend
Another False Childhood Friend

THE MISCELLANEOUS

A Servant Girl
A Maid
Malchus' Kinsmen
Good Thief
Bad Thief
Young Man
Cleopas

THE CROWDS

The Multitudes
The Pharisees
The Sadducees
The Money Changers
Dove Peddlers
Sinful Shephards
Children's Chorus
Roman Mongrels

Scene – Jerusalem & the Garden of Gethsemene in 30 AD.

sarcophagus: coffin

grave clothes: burial shroud   *John 11: 44*
napkin: burial cloth wrapping the head.

Actus Primus - Scena Prima

[Sunday: The Gates of Jerusalem]

Enter JESUS, his DISCIPLES, and the MULTITUDES

MULTITUDES

Who is this? Who is this? Is this Jesus
Whom rais'd Lazarus from his sarcophagus†?
The prophet of Nazareth of Galilee!
Witnesses there art: Martha and Mary!

MARTHA AND HER SISTER MARY

Is Jesus not the Messiah foretold? 5
He that saith, "Take ye away the stone!"
He that crieth, "Lazarus, come ye hence!"
Canst the dead walk alive at Hell's expense?
And he that was dead from the tomb arose
Bound to hand and bound to foot with grave clothes†, 10
A' bound about the chin with a napkin†.

Psalm 148:1-2

Zechariah 9:9

o'er: over

florescence: state of flowering
ascents: act of ascending, moving upwards

Acts 23:6
rebuke: to scold or reprimand   *Luke 19:39*
a': and

Luke 19:40

stones: stones of Solomon's Temple

John 12:19

This we saw thine miracle with our eyes
The Pharisees to which seethe and despise!
MULTITUDES
    Hosanna to the Son of David!
    Blessed is he that cometh   15
    In the name of the Lord!
    Hosanna in the Highest!
Behold the words of the prophets hath rung!
Rejoice greatly, O daughter of Zion!
Shout, shout! O daughter of Jerusalem   20
Beholdeth, thy King cometh unto them!
He is just as He that ruleth men o'er†.
Must be just the ruling o' God in fear!
And he shall be as the dawn's florescence†,
Having salvation whenst the sun ascents†!   25
Lowly is he riding upon a mule.
A princely mount from where David shalt rule!
Brought forth 'on a colt the foal of an ass.
Lowly animal of peace through gates pass.
    Hosanna to the Son of David!   30
    Blessed is the King that cometh
    In the name of the Lord!
    Hosanna in the Highest!
SAUL (*A Pharisee, the son of a Pharisee*)
    Master. Rabbi. Rebuke† thy disciples.
    These multitudes! a storm doth stir a'† swell.   35
JESUS
    I tell thee that if these should hold their peace
    The stones† would hereupon cry for release!
PHARISEES *to themselves*
    Perceive ye how ye prevail not-a-thing?
    Beholdeth. The world is gone after him!   39

                                Exeunt

Mark 11:13-19

foreswear: to reject or renounce with determination or as upon oath

Matthew 21:18-22

Court of the Gentiles: outer court of Solomon's Temple where
Gentiles were permitted to gather.
beguile: charm away
shekel: Jewish silver coin, worth a day's wages.

Scena Secunda

[Monday: The Temple]

Enter JESUS, and his DISCIPLES

JESUS

    Fie! Leaves but no fruit thereof? Curse ye ill:

    Of thy fruit, man must hereafter foreswear[†].

DISCIPLES

    Master, fig trees doest bud in April.

    Figs doth not bloom 'till June.

To themselves

                   Doth our Lord err?   5

Enter the PHARISEES, and others.

MONEY CHANGERS

    Within this place, the Court of the Gentiles[†],

    No Roman coin shalt greedy hands beguile[†]!

    Yield the Temple tax in Shekels[†] Tyre

Leviticus 12:6

Pasch lamb: The Korban Pesach is the
lamb sacrificed during Feast of Passover.
passo'er: God passes by the blood painted doors.
bulwarked: secure by or as if by a fortification.

drachma, bekash, gerah, talent: various ancient monetary units
score: twenty
score and ten: thirty

Leviticus 14:1-4

Two day's wages, twin silver's the duty.
Within this place, the Court of the Gentiles,   10
No Roman coin shalt greedy hands beguile!
DOVE PEDDLERS
Cleanse the women as Moses once hath said,
"Whenst days of her purifying art fled.
Fulfilled for a son or for a daughter,
She shalt bring forth a lamb of the first year.   15
For a burnt offering, and a young dove,
For a sin offering, the priest thereof."
SINFUL SHEPHERDS
Pasch lamb[†]! Young and fulleth of blood. Pasch lamb!
Buyeth thy passage lamb, painteth thy jamb
With blood, only then shalt God passo'er[†]   20
Thy house; bulwarked[†] by lamb's blood painted door.
Pasch lamb! Young and fulleth of blood. Pasch lamb!
Buyeth thy passage lamb, painteth thy jamb.
MONEY CHANGERS
Drachmas[†] and bekash[†] for but a shekel!
A score[†] of gerah[†] for but a shekel!   25
For a mina, score and ten[†]. For talents[†]
Roman tender, if thou art opulent.
Drachmas and bekash for but a shekel!
A score of gerah for but a shekel!
DOVE PEDDLERS
Cleanseth the lepers as once said Moses,   30
Scour the lepers with skin diseases.
Two turtledoves such as his coins shalt bring
One is a sin, one a burnt offering.
Cleanseth the lepers as once said Moses,
Scour the lepers with skin diseases.   35

Definition	*Scripture Reference*
	Leviticus 12:6
	Isaiah 56:7
	Mark 11:15-17
	Jeremiah 7:11
	Psalm 69:8-9
swine: pig (Jewish insult)	

MONEY CHANGERS

My weights art but the same, ne'er a pretense.
Ne'er art they shaved, my scales art in balance.
My weights art but for thee, thy opulence!
Ne'er e'er shaved, hath I of thy confidence?
My weights art but the same, ne'er a pretense.   40
Ne'er art they shaved, my scales art in balance.

DOVE PEDDLERS

Rabbi, for one I give two turtledoves
One is a sin, one a burnt offer of.
Canst fulfill the Law of Moses, Rabbi
With ne're offering a blood sacrifice.   45
Rabbi, for one I give two turtledoves
One is a sin, one a burnt offer of.

JESUS

Is it not written by him Isaiah
Their burnt offering and their sacrifice?   50
Is it not written by Jeremiah
Make not my father's house of merchandise?
For it hath been written, on these walls scrawled
For mine house of prayer for they that believe
From all nations, is this house, which is called   55
By my name becometh a den of thieves!

DISCIPLES *to themselves*

I am become a stranger, my brethren.
An alien 'to my mother's children.
For the zeal of thine house hath eaten me.
Reproaches of them, falleth upon me.   60
Is it not written? Cheer! It is written!

JESUS *pulling his sword*

Swine†! Filth! Disease in the Court of Gentiles!

debased: to lower in rank, dignity
reviled: to assail with contemptuous or opprobrious language

howbeit: nevertheless
lurch: rob, cheat
scourge: whip

gilt: gold, money

trifle: a small, inconsiderable, or   *Matthew 21:14*
trifling sum of money
forsaken: deserted; abandoned; forlorn

unsuit: not appropriate for a particular purpose
treasury: treasurer

sore: the afflicted

It is sullen. Debased†! Hath been reviled†.
My Father hath provided them a place
Of worship, for Gentiles not of our race.   65
Stealeth thou their silver; howbeit† petty
Thy lurch† the Temple of its sanctity!
I cast thee out not with a scourge† of cord
But I shalt driveth thee thus with a sword.
Begone swine, filth, from my father's Temple   70
I cast thee out, I turn o'er thy tables.
O! fie! thy grovel on the ground for gilt†,
The famished doth not beg thus for fare spilt.

JESUS drives them out of the Court of Gentiles

BLIND & LAME BEGGARS
Alms! Alms for the blind a' lame. But a trifle†.
Cannot I labor for the tax, two shekels.   75
Two days wages we, the forsaken†, lack.
Rabbi, canst spare two shekels for the tax?

JESUS
Rise and walk with me, the blind and unsuit†,
Judas, my treasury†, pay their tribute.

JUDAS
But, Master, our purse is not with gold lined.   80
There art too many and we hath too few.

JESUS
Judas, thy spirit is lame. Thy soul's blind.
We hath so much whenat they hath so few.

SAUL
Cannot the Great Temple enter the sore†,
Blind and otherwise 'to the Gentile's Court.   85

JESUS
Mayest they not sacrifice to the Lord?!

Definition	*Scripture Reference*
Elias: variation of Isaiah	*Isaiah 35:5-6*
sayer: say	*Matthew 21:15-16*
	Matthew 21:16, Psalm 8:2

SAUL
    Ne'er. They canst not see nor walk on their accord.
JESUS
    Witness! The lame walk and the blind behold!
BLIND & LAME BEGGARS
       Our eyes art opened as Isaiah foretold!
       Our spines art strong, our legs art not bowed!   90
       Let the Lord our God hear our cries unfold!
          Hosanna to the Son of David!
          Blessed is he that cometh
          In the name of the Lord!
          Hosanna in the Highest.   95
MULTITUDES
       Hosanna to the Son of David!
       Blessed is he that cometh
       In the name of the Lord!
       Hosanna in the Highest.
CHILDREN'S CHORUS
       Hosanna to the Son of David!   100
       Blessed is he that cometh
       In the name of the Lord!
       Hosanna in the Highest.
SAUL
    Doth ye hear what these children sayer[†]?
    Let not children speaketh the scripture.   105
JESUS
    Yea; have ye ne'er read, Out of the mouth of babes
    And sucklings thou hast perfected thy praise.
CHILDREN'S CHORUS
       Hosanna to the Son of David!
       Blessed is he that cometh

Definition   *Scripture Reference*

In the name of the Lord!   110
Hosanna in the Highest.

MULTITUDES

Hosanna to the Son of David!
Blessed is he that cometh
In the name of the Lord!   115
Hosanna in the Highest.   116

Exeunt

Matthew 21:20

verily: in thruth, truly, indeed   *Matthew 21:21-22*
mount: mountain

surmounts: prevails over

Scena Tertia

[Tuesday: The Temple]

Enter JESUS, his DISCIPLES, and others.

PETER

 Master, the tree thou cursedst is withered away.

JESUS

 Have faith in God. For verily† I say
 Unto you. Speaketh thee unto this mount†,
 Removeth thee; be it cast into the sea.
 Ifsoe'er in thy heart no doubt surmounts†.   5
 Whate'er prayer thy saith shalt come to be.
 What things soe'er ye desire, when ye crave,
 Believe ye receive, them ye shalt amass.
 If ye forgive, our Father hath forgave.
 If not, our Father accuses thy trespasses.   10

Definition	*Scripture Reference*
	Matthew 21:23
	Matthew 21:24-25
	Matthew 21:25-26
	Matthew 21:27
	Matthew 21:28-30
	Matthew 21:31
	Matthew 21:27, 31-32

publican: a public contractor, esp one who farmed the taxes of a province

SAUL

> Tell us, Rabbi, by what authority
> Doth thou heal the blind a' lame? Who is he
> Gaveth thee this sinful authority?

JESUS

> **I wilt asketh thee one thing. Answer me:**
> **I shalt tell thee by what authority.**   15
> **The baptism of John, Was it from Heaven?**
> **Or was it an act of most mortal men?**

PHARISEES *to themselves*

> If we sayth, From Heaven, he shalt say
> Why then believe ye him not? But if say
> Us, Of men; all this multitude shalt stone
> For they believe that John, a prophet shown.   20

SAUL

> We cannot telleth whom this hath came whence.

JESUS

> **But what think ye? A certain man had two sons; and he**
> **came to the first, and said, Son, go work to day in my**
> **vineyard. He answered and said, I will not: but afterward**
> **he repented, and went. And he came to the second, and**   25
> **said likewise. And he answered and said, I go, sir: and**
> **went not. Whether of them twain did the will of his fa-**
> **ther?**

SAUL

> The first.

JESUS

> **Neither telleth I thee by whose defense;**   30
> **By whose authority I do these things.**
> **For John came unto thee, righteous sing,**
> **Harlots believeth in him, as the publicans**†.

recant: to withdraw or disavow (a statement, opinion, etc.)

Matthew 21:33-40

husbandman: a farmer

Matthew 21:41

Matthew 21:42-44

Ye see it as harlots see? Ye recant[†]!
And ye believe Him not; as thee believe   35
Me not! Thy faith, a tapestry unweaves.

Seated amongst the Multitudes

Hear is another parable: There was a certain household-
er, which planted a vineyard, and hedged it round about,
and digged a winepress in it, and built a tower, and let it
out to husbandmen[†], and went into a far country: And   40
when the time of the fruit drew near, he sent his servants to the husbandmen, that they might receive the
fruits of it. And the husbandmen took his servants, and
beat one, and killed another, and stoned another. Again,
he sent other servants more than the first: and they did   45
unto them likewise. But last of all he sent unto them his
son, saying, They will reverence my son. But when the
husbandmen saw the son, they said among themselves,
This is the heir; come, let us kill him, and let us seize on
his inheritance. And they caught him, and cast him out   50
of the vineyard, and slew him. When the lord therefore
of the vineyard cometh, what will he do unto those husbandmen?

Multitudes

He will miserably destroy those wicked men, and will let
out his vineyard unto other husbandmen, which shall ren-   55
der him the fruits in their seasons.

Jesus

Did ye never read in the scriptures, The stone which the
builders rejected, the same is become the head of the
corner: this is the Lord's doing, and it is marvellous in
our eyes? Therefore say I unto you, The kingdom of God   60
shall be taken from you, and given to a nation bringing

Definition   *Scripture Reference*

                                                Matthew 22:2-14

forth the fruits thereof. And whosoever shall fall on this
stone shall be broken: but on whomsoever it shall fall, it
will grind him to powder.

MULTITUDES

Telleth unto us yet another parable, Rabbi. 65

JESUS

The kingdom of heaven is like unto a certain king, which
made a marriage for his son, And sent forth his servants
to call them that were bidden to the wedding: and they
would not come. Again, he sent forth other servants, saying, Tell them which are bidden, Behold, I have prepared 70
my dinner: my oxen and my fatlings are killed, and all
things are ready: come unto the marriage. But they made
light of it, and went their ways, one to his farm, another
to his merchandise, and the remnant took his servants,
and entreated them spitefully, and slew them. But when 75
the king heard thereof, he was wroth: and he sent forth
his armies, and destroyed those murderers, and burned
up their city. Then saith he to his servants, The wedding
is ready, but they which were bidden were not worthy.
Go ye therefore into the highways, and as many as ye 80
shall find, bid to the marriage. So those servants went
out into the highways, and gathered together all as many
as they found, both bad and good: and the wedding was
furnished with guests. And when the king came in to see
the guests, he saw there a man which had not on a wed- 85
ding garment: And he saith unto him, Friend, how cam-
est thou in hither not having a wedding garment? And he
was speechless. Then said the king to the servants, Bind
him hand and foot, and take him away, and cast him into
outer darkness; there shall be weeping and gnashing of 90

sooth: truth   *Matthew 22:16-17*

draught: coin
tribute: a rent, tax, or the like, as that paid by a subject to a sovereign

oppugn: to call into question; dispute
impugn: to assail (a person) by words or arguments; vilify
perquisite: something demanded or due as a particular privilege

quaint: elaborately, elegantly, finely   *Matthew 19:18*
impeach: accuse, charge, challenge
homager: one who owes homage
Holy of Holies: the innermost compartment of the Jewish tabernacle, and later of the Temple, where the Ark was enshrined
ward: a division or district of a city or town, as for administrative or political purposes.
respect: pay attention to, heed   *Matthew 19:19-20*
question: argument
resolve: answer, respond to
absolve: answer, respond to   *Matthew 19:21*

quittence: due recompense, repayment, requital   *Matthew 19:21*
Creator: God

                                                                   Matthew 22:24-28

teeth. For many are called, but few are chosen.

SAUL

> Master, we knoweth all that thou art sooth[†],
> A' thou teacheth the way of God in truth.
> A' either carest thou for any man;
> For regardest thou not persons of men.   95
> Telleth us, what thinketh thou of this draught[†].
> Giveth tribute[†] unto Caesar, or not?
> Lawful? Answer! or ask us, Sanhedrin.

PHARISEES *to themselves*

> If he speaks not, they shalt crucify him
> For treason. If yea, we shalt him oppugn[†]   100
> Disloyal to his Nation. We impugn[†]
> Him falsely. His answer art perquisite[†].

JESUS

> **Why quaint[†] impeach[†] ye me, ye hypocrites.**
> **Art we Caesar's homagers[†]? Or the Lord's?**
> **Is the Holy of Holies[†] Caesar's ward[†]?**   105

PHARISEES *to themselves*

> Respect[†] our question[†], he hath no resolve[†].
> To the cross, of this canst not he absolve[†].

JESUS

> **Showeth the tribute money me. This image**
> **Is whose? And the inscription? Whose lineage?**

SAUL

> Ceasars.   110

JESUS

> Quittance[†] unto Caesar which are Caesar's.
> A' 'to the Creator[†] the Creator's.

SADDUCEES

> Master, Moses, sayeth, If a man die

Definition	Scripture Reference

espouse: marry
kinsman: brother

bairn: child in Scottish
vernal: belonging to or characteristic of youth

Matthew 22:29-33

sham: to make a false show of something; pretend.

err: to deviate from the true course, aim, or purpose

swear: bare false witness

Luke 20:39

Matthew 22:34

Matthew 22:36

Matthew 22:37-40
Mark 12:29

Barren, his brother shalt espouse† his wife
A' raiseth up seed unto his kinsman†.   115
Ere there were with us seven brethren an'
The first whenst he hath taken the barren
Of the deceased, and hath having no bairn†
Left his wife unto his vernal† brother.
The second left her a childless mother,   120
Likewise the third a' unto the seven.
Rabbi, whose wife shalt she be in Heaven?

JESUS

Ye do err. Not knoweth thee thy scripture
Nor power of God. As touching rapture:
The resurrection of the dead. Thy sham†   125
To read God's Word sayeth, "Of Abraham,
I am God, of Isaac and of Jacob.
God is not God of the dead, the life robbed,
But the living. Ye therefore do greatly err†.

SADDUCEES *to themselves*

He lieth not, of this we must not swear†.   130

To Jesus

Thou hath speaketh soothly is thy reward!

MULTITUDES

We hath most gladly the words of the Lord!

The Pharisees gather together like ravens.

JESUS

Why dost thou flock closely as a murder?

SAUL

Which is the first commandment from God heard?

JESUS

O Israel, the Lord our God is one.   135
Hear! The Lord thy God, with all thy heart love!

Mark 12:33

Lord's capital: Heaven   *Mark 12:34*

Matthew 22:42

Matthew 22:42

Matthew 22:43-46

riposte: a quick, sharp return in speech or action   *Mark 12:36-37*

Advent: the coming of Christ into the world.

hitherto: up to this time; until now

Mark 12:37

usury: interest paid for the use of money   *Luke 21:1-4*

mites: a contribution that is small but is all that a person can afford

With all thy soul, thy mind, and with thy strength,
And the second is like, namely this by length.
Thou shalt love thy neighbour as thyself love.
None other commandment greater thereof.   140
A Scribe
Well said, Master, thy truth is more than all
The whole burnt offerings and sacrifice!
Jesus
Thou art not far from the Lord's capital[†].
To the Pharisees
What sayest O scribes concerning the Christ.
Whose son be he?
Saul
                          The son of David, king.   145
Jesus
Is the Messiah not his blood's offspring?
Sayeth David in his Psalms, I riposte[†],
Is the Christ's Advent[†] by the Holy Ghost:
Sit thou thus on my right hand; till I hew
Thine enemies thy footstool. Hitherto[†]   150
David therefore himself calleth the one
His Lord and whence is he then his own son?
Sadducees
Thou hath speaketh soothly is thy reward!
Multitudes
We hath most gladly the words of the Lord!
Enter an old widow.
Jesus
Behold! how the rich cast their usury[†].   155
How of the rich add to the treasury.
Behold! how this poor widow casts two mites[†]!

John 2:18

John 2:19

John 2:20

key: voice, words
warble: waver

John 12:21

John 12:23-28

How her share is the greater sacrifice.
All they add in of their luxuriance.
She didst cast all of her meek abundance.   160
Seest thou these great buildings? Not one stone
Halt be left 'on another; down all thrown!

PHARISEES

Rabbi, what signs shewest thou unto us?

JESUS

I shalt destroy this temple and in three
Days, yea, upon the third raise it up thus.   165

SAUL

Fie! thou no prophet. Thy insanity!
Two score and six, this temple in building!
Wilt thou rear it up again in three days?!?

JESUS

Your key† doth not warble† understanding,
But your mouth hath sang the words. Have thy faith!   170
This understanding shalt yet come in time.

A GREEK

Sir, we would seeth Jesus, the Rabbi!

JESUS

The glory of the son of man is nigh.
Except a corn of wheat fall on the field;
If shouldst it die, bringeth it forth much yield.   175
He that so loveth his life shalt lose it.
He that hateth; eternal life choose it.
If any man serveth me, let him chase,
And where I am, there shalt also my slave
Be, and in him will my Father honour.   180
Troubled my soul is. Save me from this hour,
Father? But for this cause came I this age.

John 12:28

John 12:30-32

John 12:34

John 12:35

Numbers 23:19

Matthew 23:2-39

aver: to assert or affirm with confidence; declare in a positive or

Father? Father! I glorify thy name!

VOICE OF GOD

I have both glorified it! And will glorify it again!

JESUS

This voice? Not for I, but for thine own sake   185
Cometh this voice so might the earth doeth quake!
Now is the judgment of this world: Satan
Is cast out. Lift me up, I draw all men!

SAUL

We have heard that Christ abideth fore'er.
Are thou this son of man we should lift in air?   190

JESUS

Walketh while ye have the light to showeth.
In gloom, knoweth not whither ye goeth!
While ye have light, believeth ye in the light,
That ye may be called the children of light.

SAUL

Moses sayeth that, God is not a man   195
Nor the son of man. Ye art the Satan!

JESUS

The Pharisees doth sit in Moses' seat:
Therefore whatsoe'er they bid you to heed,
And do; nay, for they sayeth and do not!
Thy observance of the law is for naught!   200
Woe unto you, Pharisees, hypocrites!
For ye shut up heaven against remit:
For ye neither go in, neither suffer
Ye them that are deserving to enter!
Woe unto you, ye blind guides, ye babble,   205
Whosoever shall swear by the temple,
'Tis not-a-thing but whosoever aver†

peremptory manner

lorn: godforsaken

By the gold of the temple is a debtor!
Ye fools and blind: for whether is more bold
The temple that sanctifieth the gold?   210
Or the gold? Woe unto you, Pharisees.
For ye are like unto whited sepulchres,
Which indeed appear beautiful as interred,
But findeth within full of dead men's bones.
And of all the uncleanness. Doth ye atone?   215
Ye art most outwardly exemplory
But within ye are full of iniquity.
Woe unto you, Pharisees, hypocrites!
Because ye build the tombs of the prophets,
And garnish the sepulchres of the pure,   220
If we had been in the days of our fathers,
We would not have been partakers with them
In the blood of the prophets. Ye children
Of them which killed the prophets. Ye serpents
Ye generation of vipers! repent!   225
How ye escape the damnation of hell?
I send unto ye prophets, to foretell
And wise men, and scribes: and some of them ye purge
And crucify; and some of them shall ye scourge
O Jerusalem, O Jerusalem,   230
Thou killest the prophets, and stonest them
Which art sent 'to thee in thy cowardice.
Behold, your house is but left lorn†;
For I sayeth unto you, Blessed is
He that cometh in the name of the Lord.   235

Exeunt

Definition   *Scripture Reference*

Luke 9:10-17

A𝑐𝑡us Secundas - Scena Prima

[Wednesday: The Palace of Caiaphas]

Enter CAIAPHAS and the PHARISEES, and others

WITNESS TO THE CONTROL OF NATURE

And they went aside privately into a desert place belonging to the city called Bethsaida. And the people, when they
knew it, followed him: and he received them, and spake
unto them of the kingdom of God, and healed them that
had need of healing. And when the day began to wear away,   5
then came the twelve, and said unto him, Send the multitude away, that they may go into the towns and country
round about, and lodge, and get victuals: for we are here
in a desert place. But he said unto them, Give ye them to
eat. And they said, We have no more but five loaves and   10
two fishes; except we should go and buy meat for all this
people. For they were about five thousand men. Then he

Mark 1:40-44

Mark 10:46-52

took the five loaves and the two fishes, and looking up to
heaven, he blessed them, and brake, and gave to the disciples to set before the multitude. And they did eat, and   15
were all filled: and there was taken up of fragments that
remained to them twelve baskets.

WITNESS TO THE HEALING OF THE LEPER

And there came a leper to him, beseeching him, and kneel-
ing down to him, and saying unto him, If thou wilt, thou
canst make me clean. And Jesus, moved with compassion,   20
put forth his hand, and touched him, and saith unto him, I
will; be thou clean. And as soon as he had spoken, immediately the leprosy departed from him, and he was cleansed.
And he straitly charged him, and forthwith sent him away;
And saith unto him, See thou say nothing to any man: 25
but go thy way, shew thyself to the priest, and offer for
thy cleansing those things which Moses commanded, for a
testimony unto them.

WITNESS TO THE HEALING OF THE BLIND

And they came to Jericho: and as he went out of Jericho
with his disciples and a great number of people, blind Bar-   30
timæus, the son of Timæus, sat by the highway side beg-
ging. And when he heard that it was Jesus of Nazareth, he
began to cry out, and say, Jesus, thou Son of David, have
mercy on me. And many charged him that he should hold
his peace: but he cried the more a great deal, Thou Son   35
of David, have mercy on me. And Jesus stood still, and
commanded him to be called. And they call the blind man,
saying unto him, Be of good comfort, rise; he calleth thee.
And he, casting away his garment, rose, and came to Jesus.
And Jesus answered and said unto him, What wilt thou   40
that I should do unto thee? The blind man said unto him,

Mark 5:1-13

legion: a division of the Roman army, usually comprising 3000 to 6000 soldiers

Luke 8:41-56

Lord, that I might receive my sight. And Jesus said unto
him, Go thy way; thy faith hath made thee whole. And immediately he received his sight, and followed Jesus in the
way.   45

Witness to the Casting Out of Demons

And they came over unto the other side of the sea, into the
country of the Gadarenes. there met him out of the tombs
a man with an unclean spirit, Who saw Jesus afar off, he
ran and worshipped him, And cried with a loud voice, and
said, What have I to do with thee, Jesus, thou Son of the   50
most high God? I adjure thee by God, that thou torment
me not. For he said unto him, Come out of the man, thou
unclean spirit. And he asked him, What is thy name? And
he answered, saying, My name is Legion†: for we are many.
And all the devils besought him, saying, Send us into the   55
swine, that we may enter into them. And forthwith Jesus
gave them leave. And the unclean spirits went out, and en-
tered into the swine: and the herd ran violently down a
steep place into the sea, (they were about two thousand;)
and were choked in the sea.   60

Witness to the Resurrection of the Dead

And, behold, there cometh one of the rulers of the syna-
gogue, Jairus by name; and when he saw him, he fell at his
feet, And besought him greatly, saying, My little daughter lieth at the point of death: I pray thee, come and lay
thy hands on her, that she may be healed; and she shall   65
live. And Jesus went with him; and much people followed
him, and thronged him. There came from his house certain which said, Thy daughter is dead: why troublest thou
the Master any further? As soon as Jesus heard the word
that was spoken, he saith him, Be not afraid, only believe.   70

John 11:46-48

question: argue

John 11:49-50

John 3:1-21

And he saweth the tumult, and them that wept and wailed
greatly. And when he was come in, he saith unto them,
Why make ye this ado, and weep? the damsel is not dead,
but sleepeth. And they laughed him to scorn. But when he
had put them all out, he taketh the father and the mother   75
of the damsel, and them that were with him, and entereth
in where the damsel was lying. And he took the damsel by
the hand, and said unto her, Talitha cumi; which is, being
interpreted, Damsel, I say unto thee, arise. And straightway the damsel arose, and walked; for she was of the age   80
of twelve years. And they were astonished with a great as-
tonishment.

Exit witnesses

PHARISEES

What do we? for many miracles from him
If we let him alone, be he forsaken,
All Judeau will believeth him the Christ.   85
Forthwith, the vile Romans shalt be enticed
To stealeth our place and our nation;
Which is our most sacred right, ne'er question†!

CAIAPHAS

Ye know not-a-thing at all. Consider this!
Is not it judicious one man should fall   90
And the whole of our nation not perish!
Should not Jesus die for the nation all?

NICODEMUS

There I was, a man of the Pharisees, named Nicodemus,
a ruler of the Jews: I came to Jesus by night, and said unto
him, Rabbi, we know that thou art a teacher come from   95
God: for no man can do these miracles that thou doest,
except God be with him. Jesus answered and said unto me,

Verily, verily, I say unto thee, Except a man be born again, he cannot see the kingdom of God. I saith unto him, How can a man be born when he is old? can he enter the second time into his mother's womb, and be born? Jesus answered me, Verily, verily, I say unto thee, Except a man be born of water and of the Spirit, he cannot enter into the king-dom of God. That which is born of the flesh is flesh; and that which is born of the Spirit is spirit. Marvel not that I said unto thee, Ye must be born again. I answered and said unto him, How can these things be? Jesus answered and said unto me, Art thou a master of Israel, and knowest not these things? Verily, verily, I say unto thee, We speak that we do know, and testify that we have seen; and ye re-ceive not our witness. If I have told you earthly things, and ye believe not, how shall ye believe, if I tell you of heavenly things? And no man hath ascended up to heaven, but he that came down from heaven, even the Son of man which is in heaven. And as Moses lifted up the serpent in the wilderness, even so must the Son of man be lifted up: That whosoever believeth in him should not perish, but have eternal life. For God so loved the world, that he gave his only begotten Son, that whosoever believeth in him should not perish, but have everlasting life. For God sent not his Son into the world to condemn the world; but that the world through him might be saved. He that believeth on him is not condemned: but he that believeth not is condemned already, because he hath not believed in the name of the only begotten Son of God. And this is the condemnation, that light is come into the world, and men loved darkness rather than light, because their deeds were evil. For every one that doeth evil hateth the light, neither

Isaiah 45:5

Isaiah 44:6

Daniel 9:24-26

civic: city.

quarried: abundant source *(from which desolation comes)*
folly-fallen: stooping to foolishness

cometh to the light, lest his deeds should be reproved. But
he that doeth truth cometh to the light, that his deeds may   130
be made manifest, that they are wrought in God.

SAUL

Answer! how can God the Father be the son
And the Spirit? I tell you, God is One!
God spake, And see no, even I, am He,
That I, there is no god even with me!   135
I am the first and the last is the Lord
And besides Me there is no God, He implored!
God is the Lord and there is no other.
A false prophet but is Satan's brother!
There can ne'er be a Holy Trinity!   140
Jesus! the Son of God? Insanity.

NICODEMUS

Daniel the dreamer sayeth, seventy weeks
Are 'on thy people and holy civic[†].
To end thy sins, finish thy trangression
Iniquity's reconciliation,   145
To bringeth everlasting rightesousness;
Seal up the vision a' reverance
O' prophecy, anoint the most divine.
Seven and threescore and two troubless times;
Howbeit after threescore and two cut off   150
Shalt the Messiah be and the Lord shalt scoff
At the destruction of the sanctuary
And end all the desolations quarried[†].
Blind folly-fallen[†]. We art days of seven
From whence the Lord our God restores heaven!   155

SAUL

Pharisees, have thee of thy faith rescued!

Isaiah 11:12

Isaiah 27:12-13

Matthew 5:17

(Fulfilled in Matthew 2: 1,5-6) Micah 5:2

(Fulfilled in John 1:1,14) Micah 5:2

(Fulfilled in Matthew 10:34-35) Micah 7:6

(Fulfilled in Luke 1:17) Malachi 4:5

(Fulfilled in Matthew 11:7-11) Malachi 3:1

procedure: course, way

(Fulfilled in Matthew 1:1) Isaiah 9:6-7

He halt told untruths; thy faith he askews.
The Prophets hath foretold the Messiah!
He is not whom is expected by us.
He shalt set up an ensign, sayeth Isaiah.   160
Assembling the outcasts doth the Messiah
Knot together to Judah the dispersed
And from all the four corners of the earth!
Isaiah sayeth, Fear not, Assyria
I bringeth thy seed from Babylonia.   165
I wilt say to the north, Give it!
Keep not back thee from the land of Egypt.
Bringeth my sons from far, back to their birth,
And my daughters from the ends of the earth!
Jesus is not the Messiah, foretold.   170
We a scattered people are. His lies are bold!

Nicodemus
Did the Rabbi not say, Doth not infer
I come to abolish the law, but to observe
The fulfillment of the law and prophets.
These are the Messiah's accomplishments: 175
Micah spake, But thou, Beth-lehem,
Though thou be little amongst the thousands.
Out of thee He come, King of Israel.
Whose going forth from old, from immortal.
For the son dishonoureth the father,   180
The daughter riseth up 'gainst her mother.
Malachi spake, Behold, Isaiah sent I.
The great and dreadful day of Adonai.
Behold, I sendeth thee my messenger,
He shalt make for Him straight the procedure†.   185
Isaiah spake, Upon the throne of David,

(Fufilled in Matthew 1:18, 23) Isaiah 7:14
Immanuel: literally "God is with us." *(in Matthew 21:42) Isaiah 28:16*

haste: hurry or rush
(Fulfilled in 1 Peter 2:8) Isaiah 8:14-15

gin: trap
well: lightly
(Fulfilled in Matthew 4:15) Isaiah 9:1

(Fulfilled in Juke 9:22, 17:25) Isaiah 53:3

(Fulfilled in Matthew 11:5) Isaiah 61:1,3

(Fulfilled in Matthew 2:18) Jeremiah 31:15

(Fulfilled in Matthew 21:5) Zechariah 9:9

(Fulfilled in 26:15) Zechariah 11:12

(Fulfilled in John 13:21) Psalm 41:9

eagle: symbol for Rome displayed on banners

Performeth the Lord of hosts art rabid.
And His title shalt be called Wonderful
Prince of Peace, the Mighty God, Counseller.
Behold, a Virgin shalt conceive a scoin,   190
Nameth him Immanuel†. In Zion
I lay for a foundation a tired stone,
He believeth shalt not make haste† alone.
And he shalt be for a home of defence,
But a stone of stumbling, rock of offence.   195
For a gin†, for a snare to Jerusalem.
And many shalt stumble, fall, be broken.
When at the first he well† afflicts the land
Of Zebulun, Naphtali, Jordan.
He is despised and of men rejected   200
A man of sorrows, with grief acquainted.
He preacheth good tidings unto the meek.
Proclaim liberty to the captives bleak;
Rent the prison to them that which are bound,
To appoint 'to them that mourn in Zion.   205
Jeremie spake, Lamentation for children
And bitter weeping for her Beth-lehem.
Zechariah spake, Rejoice Jerusalem
Thy king comes, just is He with salvation.
Brought forth 'on a colt the foal of an ass.   210
Lowly animal of peace through gates pass.
Giveth him a price, and if not forbear,
Weighed price of a score and ten of silver.
David spake, Mine own friend, whom I trusted
Lifteth his heel 'gainst me whom sopped my bread.   215
SAUL
Hath he risen 'gainst Rome, o'erthrown the eagle†?

Ezekiel 37:27-28

Should not he judge amongst all the nations?
And should not he rebuke many peoples?
And swords into plowshares forged by legions?
And their spears turnt into pruninghooks?   220
Hath Rome's oppression for peace, we mistook?
The Messiah shalt the Word of God spread.
The YHWH shalt be king of all creation!
And the gods of foreign lands to the dead.
One day shalt be one Lord and his name one!   225

NICODEMUS

Jesus, these prophecies, hath he not fulfilled.
He be youthful. Fulfill these might he still.
Is he not a prophet of the Lord like Elias.

SAUL

Prophecy can exist, only riseth,
When our land hath all the world's Jewry;   230
The death of Malachi end'd prophecy.
Ezekiel sayeth, my tabernacle
Shalt be. I their God. They my multitude
I sanctify. Thy enemies shackled.
From the stones of my covenant are hewd.   235
Didst Herod not build the place of Solomon.
Is Herod the Messiah we fawn on?
Herod maketh peace with our enemies.
Returneth Jewry to our sanctuary.
God liveth in the Holy of Holies.   240
This prophecy is but Herod's solely.
Herod, by decree of the Roman Dogs
Is the "King of the Jews". Thy not agog!

NICODEMUS

Fie! O! scribe, ye twist the Lord's word.

Deuteronomy 13:1-9

yesternight: yesterday evening

Fulfillment, Jesus is, of the scripture!   245
SAUL

There riseth up amongst us a prophet
A dreamer of dreams; giveth wonderment.
Thou shalt not hearken unto his bequile.
Walketh with ye the Lord will all the while,
Fear God, obey his voice, unto him cleave.   250
Serve ye him and in only him believe!
False Prophet shalt be put unto his death!
He dreams dreams, speaks ill with every breath.
He hath spake unsooths, from the Lord ye turn.
Whenst in Egypt thralled, ye had God's concern.   255
Moses spake, Thou shalt not be a gossipmonger!
Moses spake, Thou shalt not consent 'to him.
Thine eye not pity, nor 'to him hearken!
Neither shalt thou spare nor ye conceal him.
But thou shalt surely with thy stones kill him;   260
But the first upon him shalt be thy hand.
And thou shalt stone him with stones shalt he die!
The Lord thy God brought thee from Egypt land;
To the Romans must he be crucified!

NICODEMUS

By what action must we crucify him?   265
Lead us, O wise sages of the Sanhedrin!

SAUL

So, put the evil away from our midst.
Jesus is a false prophet! He's no Christ!

Enter JUDAS

JUDAS *in his madness*
From the shadows, thy debate I hath heard.
Yesternight† whilst the disciples slumbered,   270

houseman: a male servant who performs general duties in a home, hotel, etc.

Jesus took me aside and sayeth, Come,
Secrets may I teach ye no man knoweth
Or hath e'er seen. Exists there a great, boundless
Realm, no generation of angels knoweth
Or hath seen, wherefrom cometh a great and   275
Invisible Spirit no thought of heart
Hath ever comprehended and hath by
Name never called. There materialized
A cloud of great light that sayeth, Let an
Angel cometh into being as my   280
Houseman†. The Houseman, Self-Begotten
Enlightened-divine, issued from the cloud
A' four angels sprang from some other cloud
And they grew into housemen. The Houseman
Sayeth, Letteth angels come into   285
Being to serveth Him, and myriads
Of no known number came into being.
He sayeth, An aeon enlightened shalt
Come into being and he cameth into
Being. A second luminary reigned   290
Over him, with myriads of angels
Without known number. Adamas is the
Name of the first luminous cloud ere no
Angel amongst them calleth God who maketh
Seventy-two luminaries of the   295
Incorruptible generation, wherefore
Each hath three hundred sixty luminaires
Appeareth unto the same generation,
In accordance with the will of the Spirit.
The twelve aeons of twelve luminaries   300
Constitute their father of six heavens

Definition   *Scripture Reference*

For each aeon. Seventy-two heavens.
Seventy-two luminaries. For each
Of them five firmaments totaling
Three hundred sixty firmanents. Given   305
Authority over a great host of
Angels with nary a known number for
Glory and adoration of virgin
Spirits for glory and adoration
Of all the aeons and the heavens and   310
Their firmaments. This great multitude
Of those immortals calleth the cosmos
Or perdition by O! the great Father,
The luminaries and the aeaons.
In him appeareth the first man and the   315
Angel called El sayeth, "Let twelve angels
Cometh into being to rule over chaos.
From the cloud cameth an angel flashed with
Fire and defiled with blood named Nebro
Which the others calleth him Yaldabaoth.
Another, Saklas, cometh forth from the cloud.   320
Nebro called Saklas to be his houseman
And twelve angels claimed their twelve hides of land
Of heaven. Twelve kings spake with twelve angels,
The first is Seth, who shalt be called the Christ.
The second is Harmathoth, the third Galila,   325
The fourth Yobel, the fifth Adonaios.
Art these five rule over Hades and the
First of all over chaos. Then Saklas
Sayeth to his angels, Letteth us in the
Likeness and image create us humans.   330
Adam was fashioned as was his wife Eve,

Definition   *Scripture Reference*

Calleth in the cloud, Zoe. I asked Jesus,
Does the human spirit die. Jesus
Sayeth, Why this is God ordered Michael
To giveth the spirits of man as usury,   335
So they shouldst offer service, however
The Great One commandeth Gabriel to
Bequeath spirits to the great generation
With nary a ruler to rule o'er it –
That is the spirit and the soul. But God   340
Affected knowledge of Good and Evil
To be bequeathed to Adam and the men
With him, so the kings of chaos and Hades
Shalt not lord o'er them. I queried Jesus,
So what will those these generations do?   345
Verily, he chortled at me. Master,
I sayeth, why art ye chortling me.
Verily, he sayeth, I chortle not
At ye but at the err of the many stars.
Verily these six stars wander about   350
With five enemies and they all shalt be
Ruined along with their creatures. Verily,
I say to you, Judas, you will exceed
All of them. For you will sacrifice the
Man that bare me. Since he will be destroyed.   355
The image of the great generation
Of Adam shalt be exalted, for prior
To heaven, earth, and the angels of that
Generation which is from the eternal
Realms, exists. Look, you hath been told e'erything.   360
Lift thy eyes and looketh at the cloud and
The light held within and the surrounding

Definition   *Scripture Reference*

Stars. The star that leadeth thy way is your star.
Ye shalt becometh the thirteenth a' ye shalt
     Be cursed by the other generations –   365
And ye shalt cometh to rule o'er them all.

SAUL

Judas! Friend! Let us conspire to retire.   367

Exeunt

PRAISE ye the LORD. Praise, O ye servants of the LORD, praise the name of the LORD.

2 Blessed be the name of the LORD from this time forth and for evermore.

3 From the rising of the sun unto the going down of the same the LORD's name is to be praised.

4 The LORD is high above all nations, and his glory above the heavens.

5 Who is like unto the LORD our God, who dwelleth on high,

6 Who humbleth himself to behold the things that are in heaven, and in the earth!

7 He raiseth up the poor out of the dust, and lifteth the needy out of the dunghill;

8 That he may set him with princes, even with the princes of his people.

9 He maketh the barren woman to keep house, and to be a joyful mother of children. Praise ye the LORD.

Scena Secunda

[Thursday: An Upperroom]

Enter JESUS and His DISCIPLES

DISCIPLES *singing Psalm 113*

> *halelu yâh halelu `abhdhêy Adonay halelu 'eth-shêm Adonay*
> *yehiy shêm Adonay mebhorâkh mê`attâh ve`adh-`olâm*
> *mimmizrach-shemesh `adh-mebho'o mehullâl shêm Adonay*
> *râm`al-kâl-goyim Adonay `al hashâmayim kebhodho*
> *miy kayhvh.'elohêynu hammaghbiyhiy lâshâbheth*   5
> *hammashpiyliy lir'othbashâmayim ubhâ'ârets*
> *meqiymiy mê`âphâr dâl mê'ashpoth yâriym'ebhyon*
> *lehoshiybhiy `im-nedhiybhiym `im nedhiybhêy `ammo*
> *moshiybhiy `aqereth habbayith 'êm-habbâniym semêchâh halelu-yâh*

ANDREW

> Was not I a disciple of the Baptist?   10
> Hath I not yearned for the coming of Christ?

Matthew 16:18
Matthew 14:29

Matthew 14:30
Mark 9:1-8

Matthew 9:18-26

John 1:46

John 11:16

Of ye disciples, I was but the first!

PETER

I am the rock on which is built His church!
I walked on water. Trust is my reknown.

JAMES THE GREATER

Ha! swifty fled thy faith; to the brisk sea drown!   15
Was not I there with thee and my brother
When our Lord Jesus was transfigured?
Saweth Moses Lawgiver a' Elias
A' radiant light from the Messiah.
Heard not I the voice of the Blessed God,   20
My beloved Son, am I pleased, to Him laud!

JOHN

Am not I, John, called by Him the Beloved,
Didsn't not I find this chamber for Passo'er.
Who can claim the sight of Jairus' daughter
Resurrected: traversing death's water.   25

BARTHOLOMEW

Am not I call'd disciple of the Baptist?

JAMES THE LESSER

Didst ye not say no good comes from Nazareth?

THOMAS

I spake, Let us go! we may die with him!

JAMES THE LESSER

Ye question, argue, a' doubt is thy sin!

JUDAS

I believeth the Messiah wields a sword!   30
Shalt I force His hand to fulfill the Word!?
To extirpate the weeds of Roman dogs
From a militant Messiah! agog!

Definition	Scripture Reference
	John 13:1
	John 13:6
	John 13:7
	John 13:8
	John 13:8
	John 13:9
	John 13:11
	Matthew 26:21
	Matthew 26:22

MATTHEW
    I shalt of the Good News be chronicler.
JAMES THE LESSER
    Fie! ye art the bane! a tax collector!   35
JESUS
    That I should depart this world, my hour is come;
    My own in this world, 'to the end I love.
    Father hath given all, his hands to laud.
    I hath come from God, and return to God.
PETER
    Lord, dost thou, no servant, ye wash my feet.   40
JESUS
    What I do thou knowest not 'fore we eat.
    But thou shalt know of this afterart.
PETER
    Wash not.
JESUS
               If I wash not, thou hast no part.
PETER
    Lord, not my feet only, but my hands and head.
JOHN
    Lord, not my feet only, so my heart nar' dread.   45
JUDAS
    Lord, not my feet only, from soil to sheen.
JESUS
    Judas, my disciple, ye art not all clean.
    Verily, O my disciples, I say,
    One of you, eateth here, will me betray.
DISCIPLES *repeating amongst themselves*
    Lord, is it I? Is it I, Lord?   50

Matthew 26:23-24

sop: a piece of solid food, as bread, for dipping in liquid food

Matthew 26:25

Matthew 26:25

John 13:36

Luke 22:33

smite: to strike or hit hard, with   *Zechariah 13:7*
or as with the hand, a stick, or other weapon

Mark 14:29

palpable-gross: obviously clumsy, painfully ignorant
imperseverant: stubborn, obstinate
                                                          Mark 14:30

thrice: three times

gainsay: deny, refuse   *Mark 14:31*
imbrue: pierce, stab, stain with blood

PETER

    Lord, who is it?

JESUS

    My prophesies, Peter, hath ye not heard?

    He that dippeth his sop† in bitter herb

    Whenst I dippeth my sop will me betray.

    His life's book shalt be written full of scorn.   55

JUDAS

    Rabbi, is it I?

JESUS

                  Are your words ye say.

    Good would that man if he had ne'er been born.

    Whither I go, thou canst not follow thy Lord

    But thou shalt follow thy Lord afterward.

PETER

    Lord, where ye lead, I walk with ye breadth   60

    Both into a prison and to my death.

JESUS

    Zechariah sayeth, Smite† the Shepherd

    And all of his sheep to the wind scattered.

PETER

    E'en if the others art made to stumble,

    I will not be. Proud of ye, nar' humble.   65

JESUS

    Thy protestations are palpable-gross†;

    Imperseverant† pride is grandiose!

    I tell thee, Peter, the cock shalt not crow twice

    Before ye deny ye knowest me thrice†.

PETER

    I'll no gainsay†! this sword my breast imbrue†.   70

    If to die with You, I shalt ne'er deny You!

spleenful: furious, hot-headed, passionate   *Luke 22:31-32*

avail: to be of use or value to; profit; advantage

bride: drench, dip

speed: success, fortune, good luck/carry out, expedite

gall: impudence

machination: plotting, intrigue, scheming

malefaction: evil-doing, criminal act

malignancy: evil influence, inauspicious character

painfully: diligency, taking great pains

guiled: cunning, deceit, treachery

> *13 I will take the cup of salvation, and call upon the name of the LORD.*
> *14 I will pay my vows unto the LORD now in the presence of all his people.*
> *15 Precious in the sight of the LORD is the death of his saints.*
> *16 O LORD, truly I am thy servant; I am thy servant, and the son of thine handmaid: thou hast loosed my bonds.*
> *17 I will offer to thee the sacrifice of thanksgiving, and will call upon the name of the LORD.*
> *18 I will pay my vows unto the LORD now in the presence of all his people,*
> *19 In the courts of the LORD's house, in the midst of thee,*   *Luke 22:15-16*
> *O Jerusalem. Praise ye the LORD.*

Mark 14:25

Matthew 26:26-28

DISCIPLES *so say them all*
JESUS

> Spleenful† Simon! I have prayed for avail†;
> Studied hath I that your faith shouldst not fail.
> Return to me and strengthen your brethren.

Aside to JUDAS

> Judas, thy bribed† thy sop whenst I dippest.   75
> What thou dost do, dost thou with speed† doest.
> Thy gall† wit' Saul; pursue thy machination†.
> Thy heart pronounces its malefaction†.
> Thy soul infected with malignancy†.
> Painfully† seek through ye this guiled† fancy.   80

Exit JUDAS

DISCIPLES *singing Psalm 116:13-19*

> *kos-yeshu`oth 'esâ'ubheshêm Adonay 'eqrâ'*
> *nedhâray layhvh 'ashallêm neghdhâh-nâ'lekhol-`ammo*
> *yâqâr be`êynêy Adonay hammâvthâhlachasiydhâyv*
> *'ânnâh Adonay kiy-'aniy `abhdekha 'aniy-`abhdekhaben-*
> *'amâthekha pittachtâ lemosêrây*   85
> *lekha-'ezbach zebhach todhâhubheshêm Adonay 'eqrâ'*
> *nedhâray layhvh 'ashallêm neghdhâh-nâ'lekhol-`ammo*
> *bechatsroth bêyth Adonay bethokhêkhiy yerushâlâimhalelu-yâh*

JESUS

> With want hath I desired to eat Passo'er
> With you, my disciples before I suffer.   90
> Yea! I will not any more thereof eat
> Until I sit on God's right-handed seat.
> I wilt not drink of the fruit of the vine
> Until the kingdom of God shalt betide!
>> Take, eat: this is my body   95
>> Which is broken for you.

John 14:1

John 14:6

O GIVE *thanks unto the LORD; for he is good: because his mercy endureth for ever.*

2 Let Israel now say, that his mercy endureth for ever.

3 Let the house of Aaron now say, that his mercy endureth for ever.

4 Let them now that fear the LORD say, that his mercy endureth for ever.

5 I called upon the LORD in distress: the LORD answered me, and set me in a large place.

6 The LORD is on my side; I will not fear: what can man do unto me?

7 The LORD taketh my part with them that help me: therefore shall I see my desire upon them that hate me.

8 It is better to trust in the LORD than to put confidence in man.

9 It is better to trust in the LORD than to put confidence in princes.

10 All nations compassed me about: but in the name of the LORD will I destroy them.

11 They compassed me about; yea, they compassed me about: but in the name of the LORD I will destroy them.

12 They compassed me about like bees; they are quenched as the fire of thorns: for in the name of the LORD I will destroy them.

13 Thou hast thrust sore at me that I might fall: but the LORD helped me.

14 The LORD is my strength and song, and is become my salvation.

15 The voice of rejoicing and salvation is in the tabernacles of the righteous: the right hand of the LORD doeth

This do in remembrance of me.
Take, drink: this is my blood
The blood of a New Covenant
Which is shed for you.   100
This do in remembrance of me.
Lettest not ye heart nor spirit be grieved.
Ye believe in God, in me then believe.
For I am the way, the truth, and the life,
No man cometh unto the Father but by Christ.   105

DISCIPLES *singing Psalm 118 while Jesus laments His soliloquy*

hodhu layhvh kiy-thobh kiy le`olâm chasdo
yo'mar-nâ'yisrâ'êl kiy le`olâm chasdo
yo'mru-nâ' bhêyth-'aharon kiy le`olâmchasdo
yo'mru-nâ' yir'êy Adonay kiy le`olâm chasdo
min-hammêtsar qârâ'thiy yâh `anâniy bhammerchâbh yâh   110
Adonay liylo' 'iyrâ' mah-ya`aseh liy `âdhâm
Adonay liy be`ozerây va'aniy'er'eh bhesone'ây
thobb lachasoth bayhvh mibbethoach bâ'âdhâm
thobhlachasoth bayhvh mibbethoach bindhiybhiym
kol-goyim sebhâbhuniybeshêm Adonay kiy 'amiylam   115
sabbuniy gham-sebhâbhuniy beshêmAdonay kiy 'amiylam
sabbuniy khidhbhoriym do`akhu ke'êshqotsiym beshêm Adonay

kiy 'amiylam

dachoh dhechiythaniy linpol.vayhvh `azârâniy
`azziy vezimrâth yâh vayhiy-liy liyshu`âh   120
qol rinnâh viyshu`âh be'oholêy tsaddiyqiym yemiyn Adonay`osâh châyil
yemiyn Adonay romêmâh yemiyn Adonay`osâh châyil
lo' `âmuth kiy-'echyeh va'asappêr ma`asêy yâh
yassor yisseranniy yâh velammâveth lo' nethânâniy
pithchu-liysha`arêy-tsedheq 'âbho'-bhâm 'odheh yâh   125
zeh-hasha`ar layhvhtsaddiyqiym yâbho'u bho

valiantly.

16 The right hand of the LORD is exalted: the right hand of the LORD doeth valiantly.

17 I shall not die, but live, and declare the works of the LORD.

18 The LORD hath chastened me sore: but he hath not given me over unto death.

19 Open to me the gates of righteousness: I will go into them, and I will praise the LORD:

20 This gate of the LORD, into which the righteous shall enter.

21 I will praise thee: for thou hast heard me, and art become my salvation.

22 The stone which the builders refused is become the head stone of the corner.

23 This is the LORD's doing; it is marvellous in our eyes.

24 This is the day which the LORD hath made; we will rejoice and be glad in it.   *John 17:1-24*

25 Save now, I beseech thee, O LORD: O LORD, I beseech thee, send now prosperity.

26 Blessed be he that cometh in the name of the LORD: we have blessed you out of the house of the LORD.

27 God is the LORD, which hath shewed us light: bind the sacrifice with cords, even unto the horns of the altar.

28 Thou art my God, and I will praise thee: thou art my God, I will exalt thee.

29 O give thanks unto the LORD; for he is good: for his mercy endureth for ever.

'odhekha kiy `aniythâniy vattehiy-liy liyshu`âh
'ebhen mâ'asu habboniym hâythâh lero'sh pinnâh
mê'êthAdonay hâythâh zo'th hiy' niphlâ'th be`êynêynu
zeh-hayyom`âsâh Adonay nâghiylâh venismechâh bho   130
'ânnâ' Adonayhoshiy`âh nâ' 'ânnâ' Adonay hatsliychâh nâ'
bârukh habbâ'beshêm Adonay bêrakhnukhem mibbêyth Adonay
'êlAdonay vayyâ'er lânu 'isru-chagh ba`abhothiym `adh-qarnoth-
hammizbêach
'êliy 'attâh ve'odhekhâ 'elohay 'aromemekhâ   135
hodhu layhvh kiy-thobh kiy le`olâm chasdo

JESUS *while the Disciples sing Psalm 118*
    Father, glorify thy Son, that thy son
    Too may glorify thee, the hour is come.
    Thou hast given him power o'er all flesh,
    Endless life to as many through the Pasch   140
    Lamb of God through whom shalt be sacrificed
    They might know thee Only True God and Christ,
    Whom thou hast sent. Glory to thee on earth.
    Thou gavest me tasks, I hath crowned thy work.
    O Father, glorify thou me with thine own share   145
    The glory I had before the world inhered.
    Manifested they name unto the men
    They were thine, and thou gavest to me them;
    Which thou gavest to me out of the world:
    Obeyed hath them, and they have kept thy word   150
    They know things given me are of thee.
    Words I gavest them, Words thou gavest me.
    Receiv'd them the words, that I came from thee
    They didst believe that thou didst send of me.
    Not for the world I pray. I pray for them   155

Definition   *Scripture Reference*

For which thou hast given me; they are thine.
Glory! all mine are thine and all thine are mine.
No more in the world now am I. I came
To thee, Holy Father, keep thine own name.
Those hast given me and they may be one.   160
As we are; the Father, the Ghost, the Son
Of Perdition; that scripture might be laud.
Thy name I kept them those gavest me of God!
The world hell-hated them given thy word.
They are not, as I am not of the world.   165
Shouldest thy not take them, I pray, out of life.
But thou shouldest keep them from evil and strife.
Through thy truth sanctify them: thy Gospel!
And for their sakes I sanctify myself.
Neither these alone, I pray to be heard   170
But for them which believe me through their word!
All may be one; O Father, art in me.
May they be one in us, as I in thee.
Which thou gavest of glory to the Son
Given I to them; that they may be one.   175
I in them, thou in me perfect in one.
Thou hast loved them, as thou hast loved the Son.
O righteous Father, they hath known thee not:
But I hath known thee and they know thou sent me.
I declare thy name, they will declare thee!   180
Further the Love wherewith thou hast loved me
May be in them, and I in them and thee!   182

Exeunt

Matthew 26:36-39

grevious: sorrowful, heavy, grave, serious
tarry: stay, remain, linger
Abba: Hebrew for "daddy."

grail: chalice
sup: drink; to eat the evening meal; have supper

Psalm 22:1-31

Scena Tertia

[Thursday: The Garden of Gethsemane]

Enter JESUS while his DISCIPLES sleep.

JESUS

    Sitteth here whilst I go a' pray o'er there.

    Gravely grevious[†] is my soul, e'en to fear

    To death. Tarry[†] ye here, keep o'er the Son.

    O! woe! Abba[†], if it be possible let this cup

    Passeth from me: ne'ertheless Thy will be done,   5

    Not as I will. I wilt from thy grail[†] sup[†].

Lamenting Psalm 22

    My God, my God, why hast thou forsaken me?

    Why art thou so far from helping me,

    And from the words of my roaring?

    O my God, I cry in the daytime, but thou hearest not;   10

    And in the night season, and am not silent.

But thou art holy, O thou that inhabitest the praises of Israel.
Their fathers trusted in thee: they trusted,
And thou didst deliver them.
They cried unto thee, and were delivered: 15
They trusted in thee, and were not confounded.
But I am a worm, and no man;
A reproach of men, and despised of the people.
All they that see me laugh me to scorn:
They shoot out the lip, they shake the head, saying,   20
He trusted on the LORD that he would deliver him:
Let him deliver him, seeing he delighted in him.
But thou art he that took me out of the womb:
Thou didst make them hope
When I was upon my mother's breasts.   25
I was cast upon thee from the womb:
Thou art my God from my mother's belly.
Be not far from me; for trouble is near;
For there is none to help.
Many bulls have compassed me: 30
Strong bulls of Bashan have beset me round.
They gaped upon me with their mouths,
As a ravening and a roaring lion.
I am poured out like water,
And all my bones are out of joint: 35
My heart is like wax;
It is melted in the midst of my bowels.
My strength is dried up like a potsherd;
And my tongue cleaveth to my jaws;
And thou hast brought me into the dust of death.   40
For dogs have compassed me:
The assembly of the wicked have inclosed me:

Definition   *Scripture Reference*

Matthew 26:40-42

Matthew 26:43

They shalt pierce my hands and my feet.
I may tell all my bones: they look and stare upon me.
They shalt part my garments among them,   45
And cast lots upon my vesture.
What, couldst ye not watch with me one hour?
Watch and pray, ye enter not into lure.
Thy spirit, my Disciples, is willing.
Erelong the flesh, forsooth, is uncertain.   50
O! my Abba, if it be possible let this cup
Passeth from me: ne'ertheless Thy will be done,
Not as I will. I wilt from thy grail sup.
But be not thou far from me, O LORD:
O my strength, haste thee to help me.   55
Deliver my soul from the sword;
My darling from the power of the dog.
Save me from the lion's mouth:
For thou hast heard me from the horns of the unicorns.
I will declare thy name unto my brethren: 60
In the midst of the congregation will I praise thee.
Ye that fear the LORD, praise him;
All ye the seed of Jacob, glorify him;
And fear him, all ye the seed of Israel.
For I hath not despised nor abhorred   65
The affliction of the afflicted;
Neither hath ye hid ye face from me;
But when I cried unto ye, ye heard.
What, couldst ye not watch with me one hour?
Watch and pray, ye enter not into lure.   70
O! my Abba, if it be possible let this cup
Passeth from me: ne'ertheless Thy will be done,
Not as I will. I wilt from thy grail sup.

roughed: acting with or characterized by unnecessary violence
knot: company, band, assembly
trespass: wrong, offence, injustice, crime
garboil: trouble, disturbance, commotion   *Luke 22:47*

                                                                Luke 22:48
onuses: duty, burden of proof, a difficult or disagreeable obliga-
tion, task, burden, etc   *Luke 22:50*

                                                                Matthew 26:52-54

My praise shall be of thee in the great congregation:
I will pay my vows before them that fear him.   75
The meek shall eat and be satisfied:
They shall praise the LORD that seek him:
Your heart shall live for ever.
All the ends of the world shall remember
And turn unto ye, LORD: 80
And all the kindreds of the nations shall worship before thee.
For the kingdom is the LORD's:
And he is the governor among the nations.
All they that be fat upon earth shall eat and worship:
All they that go down to the dust shall bow before him: 85
And none can keep alive his own soul. A seed shall serve him;
It shall be accounted to the Lord for a generation.
They shall come, and shall declare his righteousness
Unto a people that shall be born, that he hath done this.
Sleep on now and take thy rest; it is enough.   90
The hour is come; the son of Man roughed[†]
'To a knot[†] of sinners though a trespass[†].
Rise up, lo! this garboil[†] awaked Judas.

And while he yet spake, behold a multitude, and he what was called
JUDAS, one of the twelve, went before them, and drew near unto
JESUS to kiss him.

JESUS

Judas, betrayest thou the Son of man with a kiss?
The onuses[†] of prophets be remiss?   95

Then Simon PETER having a sword drew it and smote the high
priest's servant and cut off his right ear.

Keep back! again the sword in its scabbard;
Who taketh the sword, perish whence the sword.
Suffer ye thus far.

Definition   *Scripture Reference*

And he touched MALCUS' ear and healed him.

                    To Me canst the Lord
  Giveth twelve legions? a heavenly horde!
  I, a thief? comest ye with swords and staves?   100
  Wast I not in the temple therein to save?
  But this is your hour, the power of the pit.
  Fulfilled art the scriptures of the prophets.   102

                             Exeunt

Gospel of Thomas 114

Gospel of Thomas 55

Scena Quarta

[*Thursday: The Courtyard of the Houses of Annas & Caiaphas*]

Enter JESUS, CAIAPHAS, SAUL, the PHARISEES and FALSE WITNESSES

A FALSE WITNESS

I heard his disciples sayeth, Let Mary who was possessed of demons goeth away from us for women are not worthy of life. And Jesus sayeth, Lo, I will draweth her so I wilt make her a man so that she too may becomest a living spirit which is like you men; for every woman who maketh herself a man wilt entereth into the kingdom of heaven.

A SECOND FALSE WITNESS

I heard this Jesus sayeth, He who shalt not hate his own father and mother cannot be mine disciple. And he who shalt not hate his brothers and sisters cannot carry his cross as I have, and is not worthy of me.

Definition   Scripture Reference

                                          From Infancy Gospel of Thomas

                                          From Infancy Gospel of Thomas

A FALSE CHILDHOOD FRIEND

Now when Jesus was five years old there was a great rain
upon the earth, and the child Jesus walked about therein.
And the rain was very terrible: and he gathered the water together into a pool and commanded with a word that
it should become clear: and forthwith it did so. Again, he   15
took of the clay which came of that pool and made thereof
to the number of twelve sparrows. Now it was the Sabbath day when Jesus did this among the children of the
Hebrews: and the children of the Hebrews went and said
unto Joseph his father: Lo, thy son was playing with us and   20
he took clay and made sparrows which it was not right to
do upon the Sabbath, and he hath broken it. And Joseph
went to the child Jesus, and said unto him: Wherefore hast
thou done this which it was not right to do on the Sabbath? But Jesus spread forth (opened) his hands and com-   25
manded the sparrows, saying: Go forth into the height and
fly: ye shall not meet death at any man's hands. And they
flew and began to cry out and praise almighty God!

ANOTHER FALSE CHILDHOOD FRIEND

Yea! Yea! I witnessed it. Now on another day, when Jesus
climbed up upon a house with the children, he began to   30
play with them: but one of the boys fell down through the
door out of the upper chamber and died straightway. And
when the children saw it they fled all of them, but Jesus
remained alone in the house. And when the parents of the
child which had died came they spake against Jesus saying: 35
Of a truth thou madest him fall. But Jesus said: I never
made him fall: nevertheless they accused him still. Jesus
therefore came down from the house and stood over the
dead child and cried with a loud voice, calling him by his

Matthew 26:62

Zechariah 13:7

Zechariah 13:4

howbeit: however
Adonai: Lord
aforesaid: prophesied

daub: to smear, soil, or defile

Zechariah 13:7
Zechariah 13:5-6

kine: cattle

emminence: glory   *1 Samuel 15:29*
bewail: express deep sorrow

Isaiah 2:4

name: Zeno, Zeno, arise and say if I made thee fall. And   40
on a sudden he arose and said: Nay, Lord. And when his
parents saw this great miracle which Jesus did, they glorified God, and worshipped Jesus!

CAIAPHAS

What is it these men testify 'gainst You?

JESUS *answers nothing.*

SAUL

Ye quoted the prophet, Smite the Shepherd   45
And all of his sheep to the wind scattered.
And it shalt come to pass when any
Shalt howbeit† through words false prophecy.
For thou spake lies in the name Adonai†
And it shalt come to pass in aforesaid† day   50
The prophets shalt be ashamed of thy vision.
Ye cometh to render with derision.

NICODEMUS

Ye daub† the truth. Shalt he proclaim the Word?
Awake O! sword, against this low shepherd.
I am no prophet, I am the husbandman.   55
For me to keep lean kine† is the Lord's plan.
And shalt he say? What are these wounds in ye hand?
For which I was wounded in the house of friends.

SAUL

Zebud spake, The Emminence† of Israel
A man is not for to lie nor bewail†!   60
Hath ye risen 'gainst Rome, o'erthrown the eagle?
Should not ye judge amongst all the nations?
And should not ye rebuke many peoples?
And swords into plowshares forged by legions?
And their spears turnt into pruninghooks?   65

Isaiah 11:12

Isaiah 27:12-13

Matthew 26:67
Matthew 26:68

Acts 9:4

Hath Rome's oppression for peace, we mistook?
The Messiah shalt the Word of God spread.
The YHWH shalt be king of all creation!
And the gods of foreign lands to the dead.
One day shalt be one Lord and his name one!   70
NICODEMUS
Teacher, ye speak in circles. We hath heard
These arguments. Relent! Repent thy words.
SAUL
Hath this Jesus heard of my argument?
Is this Jesus of God omnipotent?
Shalt ye set up an ensign, sayeth Isaiah.   75
Assembling the outcasts doth the Messiah
Knot together to Judah the dispersed
And from all the four corners of the earth!
Isaiah sayeth, Fear not, Assyria
I bringeth thy seed from Babylonia.   80
I wilt say to the north, Give it!
Keep not back thee from the land of Egypt.
Bringeth my sons from far, back to their birth,
And my daughters from the ends of the earth!
Jesus thou not the Messiah, foretold.   85
We a squandered people are. Thy lies are bold!
Hosea spake, Whenst Israel was a child
A' call'd my son out of Egypt exile.
We, Isreal, art the sons of God. Not thee!
SAUL strikes JESUS
Messiah? Fie! Christ to us Prophesy!   90
Whate'er is the name of he who smote thee?
JESUS
Saul! O! Saul, why persecutest thou me?

Definition	*Scripture Reference*
	Matthew 26:63
Blessed: a name of the Hebrew God	
I AM: a name of the Hebrew God	*Mark 14:62, Exodus 3:14*
Aaron's rod: a staff carried by Moses' brother Aaron, symbol of authority within the Temple.	*Mark 14:63*
	Mark 14:63
	Isaiah 45:5
	Isaiah 44:6

CAIAPHAS
>Ye I put under oath by the living God!
>Are You the Christ, the Son of the Blessed[†]?

JESUS
>I AM[†].

CAIAPHAS
>   Fraud! Striketh thee wit' Aaron's rod[†]!   95

CAIAPHAS rents his clothes.

CAIAPHAS
>What need we any further of witnesses?
>Ye hath heard the blasphemy on his breath.
>The False Christ condemned! Guilty to His death!

The PHARISEES spit on him.

SAUL
>Answer! how can God the Father be the Son
>And the Spirit? I tell you, God is One!   100
>God spake, And see no, even I, am He,
>That I, there is no god even with me!
>I am the first and the last is the Lord
>And besides Me there is no God, He implored!
>God is the Lord and there is no other.   105
>A false prophet but is Satan's brother!
>There can ne'er be a Holy Trinity!
>Jesus! the Son of God? Insanity.

>   *Exit JESUS and the TEMPLE GUARDS into the Street*

THE MULTITUDES *in the street*
>Is not the Christ foretold by Isaiah?
>Wherefore art thou, Jesus, the Messiah!   110
>Wherethrough God ye cometh to Israel:
>The children of Isaac, ne'er to Ishmael!
>Witherward salvation, we taketh thy lead.

Deuteronomy 13:1-9

lethe: oblivion

Mark 14:67, John 18:17

Mark 14:68, John 18:17

Mark 14:70, John 18:25

Jesus! Jesus! heareth our cries, we plead!
Whencesoe'er shalt our sins by Him releas'd?   115
What thinkest ye of Jesus O! Saul the priest?

SAUL *amidst the Multitudes*

There riseth up amongst us a prophet
A dreamer of dreams; giveth wonderment.
Thou shalt not hearken unto his beguile.
Walketh with ye the Lord will all the while,   120
Fear God, obey his voice, unto him cleave.
Serve ye him and in only him believe!
False Prophet shalt be put unto his lethe†!
He dreams dreams, speaks ill with every breath.
He hath spake unsooths, from the Lord ye turn.   125
Whenst in Egypt thralled, ye had God's concern.
Moses spake, Thou shalt not be a gossipmonger!
Moses spake, Thou shalt not consent 'to him.
Thine eye not pity, nor 'to him hearken!
Neither shalt thou spare nor ye conceal him.   130
But thou shalt surely with thy stones kill him;
But the first upon him shalt be thy hand.
And thou shalt stone him with stones shalt he die!
The Lord thy God brought thee from Egypt land;
To the Romans must he be crucified!   135

A SERVANT GIRL *to Peter*

And thou, also wast with Jesus of Nazareth?

PETER

I knowest not, neither understand I what thou sayeth.

The cock crows.

A MAID

Surely thou art one of them for thou art a Galilean and thy
speech agreeth thereto.

Definition	*Scripture Reference*
	Mark 14: 70, John 18:25
	John 18:26
murrain: plague, pestilence	Mark 14:71
	Mark 14:72, John 18:26
	Psalm 51:1-19

PETER

    Nay! faith. I am not.   140

MALCHUS' KINSMAN

    Did not I see thee in the garden with him? Yea! ye hath cut
    off my kinsman's ear! He is a disciple of the criminal Jesus!
    Crucify him in turn!

PETER

    A murrain† on thy words. I doth not know this Man of
    whom you speak. God shalt mend my soul if I lieth. God   145
    warrant me! I am not one with Him. A devil's name! bear
    not false witness against me. I am not nor e'er hath been
    this Man's disciple!

*The cock crows twice. PETER, in tears, runs to JESUS but the TEM-
PLE GUARDS stop him.*

PETER *continuing*

    Have mercy upon me, O God,
    According to thy lovingkindness: 150
    According unto the multitude of thy tender mercies
    Blot out my transgressions.
    Wash me throughly from mine iniquity,
    And cleanse me from my sin.
    For I acknowledge my transgressions: 155
    And my sin is ever before me.
    Against thee, thee only, have I sinned,
    And done this evil in thy sight:
    That thou mightest be justified when thou speakest,
    And be clear when thou judgest.   160
    Behold, I was shapen in iniquity;
    And in sin did my mother conceive me.
    Behold, thou desirest truth in the inward parts:
    And in the hidden part thou shalt make me to know wisdom.

Definition   *Scripture Reference*

Matthew 27:4

Purge me with hyssop, and I shall be clean: 165
Wash me, and I shall be whiter than snow.
Make me to hear joy and gladness;
That the bones which thou hast broken may rejoice.
Hide thy face from my sins,
And blot out all mine iniquities.   170
Create in me a clean heart, O God;
And renew a right spirit within me.
Cast me not away from thy presence;
And take not thy holy spirit from me.
Restore unto me the joy of thy salvation;   175
And uphold me with thy free spirit.
Then will I teach transgressors thy ways;
And sinners shall be converted unto thee.
Deliver me from bloodguiltiness,
O God, thou God of my salvation: 180
And my tongue shall sing aloud of thy righteousness.
O Lord, open thou my lips;
And my mouth shall shew forth thy praise.
For thou desirest not sacrifice; else would I give it:
Thou delightest not in burnt offering.   185
The sacrifices of God are a broken spirit:
A broken and a contrite heart, O God, thou wilt not despise.
Do good in thy good pleasure unto Zion:
Build thou the walls of Jerusalem.
Then shalt thou be pleased with the sacrifices of righteousness, 190
With burnt offering and whole burnt offering:
Then shall they offer bullocks upon thine altar.

The TEMPLE GUARDS carry JESUS away as others beat PETER.

JUDAS

I hath sinned in that I betrayed the innocent blood!

Definition	*Scripture Reference*
	Matthew 27:4
statutory: lawful	Matthew 27:6-8
maugre: in spite of	Matthew 27:9-10, Jeremiah 32:6-9
	Matthew 27:9-10

yield: hand over, give up, deliver; reward, repay; concede, acknowledge; value   *Acts 1:19*
traffic: purchase
Aceldame: the name of the field of blood purchased with Judas' money.

SAUL

> What is that to us? Hearken after good!
>> *JUDAS throws down his 30 pieces of silver and exits.*

SAUL *continuing*

> But this silver is not statutory†   195
> To put score and ten into the treasury.
> Maugre†! Is it not the price of life's blood?
> Taketh council! Needeth council! O! Lord!

NICODEMUS

> Jeremie spake, And they took score and ten
> That was the value. That was price of Him.   200
> Whom they of the Lord's children did yield†
> To traffic† Aceldama†, the potter's field.   202
>> *Exeunt*

malefactor: a person who violates the law; criminal
Prefector: governor

A&us Tertias - Scena Prima

[*Friday Morning: The Palace of Pontius Pilate*]

*Enter JESUS, PONTIUS PILATE, the PHARISEES, and
ROMAN MONGRELS*

PONTIUS PILATE

    What accusation bring you against this man?

SAUL

    If Jesus were not a malefactor[†],

    We wouldst not deliver him, Prefector[†]!

PONTIUS PILATE

    Take ye him, and judge him according to your law.

SAUL

    'Tis not hitherto our jurisdcition.   5

    To put Him to death by crucifixion.

PONTIUS PILATE

    This man is Jesus of Nazareth. Herein is he charged with

Definition	Scripture Reference
sorcery: healing with black magic	
sacrilege: blasphemy	*Mark 15:2*
sedition: treason	
Prefect: governor	*Mark 15:2, Luke 23:3*
sect: Jewish people	
	John 18:35
	John 18:36
	John 18:37
	John 18:37
forewarn: to warn in advance	
sooth: truth	
	John 18:38
fellow: brother	

sorcery[†], sacrilege[†], and sedition[†]. In the name of our most
revered and respected Tiberius Caesar, art thou the King
of the Jews?   10

JESUS

Thou sayest this thing of thyself, Prefect[†]
Or did they tell of me from my own sect[†].

PONTIUS PILATE

Am I a Jew? Thine own nation and the chief priests have
delivered thee unto me: what hast thou done?

JESUS

Prefect, my kingdom is not of this world   15
If my kingdom were of this world then would
My servants fight, I shouldst need no defense.
Woe! but now is my kingdom not from hence.

PONTIUS PILATE

Art thou a king then?

JESUS

Thou sayest that. To this end was I born.   20
Came I to bear witness; the truth forewarn[†].
That every one that heard my voice is sooth[†].

PONTIUS PILATE

What is the truth?

JESUS is silent.

PONTIUS PILATE *continuing*

Saul, speaketh thy charges against this Jew.

SAUL

We found this fellow[†] perverting the nation,   25
He art guilty 'gainst Rome of sedition!

PONTIUS PILATE.

List the charges arraigned against this man.

lazars: lepers

Hades: Greek underworld

not-a-thing: nothing

Matthew 27:13

jewry: Jewish nation   *Luke 23:5*

Luke 23:6-7

render: give

season: time   *Luke 23:8-11*

ROMAN MONGREL

The chief priests of the Sanhedrin charge this Rabbi of
their own faith with conspiring with demons during exor-
cisms. Healing lazars†, those cursed souls condemned by   30
the gods to suffer sins of a past life in this life, with sorcery
and with this same sorcery, he raiseth the dead from Ha-
des†. He claimeth to be the Son of God and a King of a
heavenly kingdom.

PONTIUS PILATE

Caesar rules as king of Judah; I am his Prefect. Wherefore   35
art thy kingdom, thy highness?

JESUS *is silent.*

PONTIUS PILATE *continuing*

Doth Ye answer not-a-thing†. Hearest thou not how many
things they witness against thee?

SAUL

He stirreth up against Rome the jewry.†
Jesus of Nazareth of Galilee.   40

PONTIUS PILATE

Sayeth thou Galilee? Whether be it this man of Galilee?
This King of the Jews is not of my jurisdiction. Let Herod,
who is rendered† by Tiberius the King of the Jews. Let him
render his verdict.

[Friday morning: The Palace of Herod Antipas]
Enter *JESUS.*

HEROD ANTIPAS

Desirous for many a season† hath I been to see thee, Je-   45
sus of Nazareth of Galilee. Exceeding glad am I. Hath
I heard many things of ye. I hope to see many miracles
done by thee. I heareth thee keepeth company with lep-

sprunt: to spring up; to germinate; to spring forward or outward

ers. Doth thy heal the lepers of their manhood whenst it
shrivels on the branch and falleth off like autumn leaves?   50
Doth thy pick from the dirt their withered worm and restore it? Come now, healer, giveth back unto my eunuch
his virility. Touch him wherein he wast untimely pruned
of the bush. Sprunt[†] from his lacking seed a great, stout,
erect oak. Heal him. Maketh him a man. Nay? I heareth   55
thee keepeth company with prostitutes. Art these harlots
thy harem, thy concubines? If ye art the King of the Jews,
where art thy queen to swell big bellied at the strike of thy
serpent. Whereat art thy heirs to propagate thy dynasty. Is
not one of thy disciples a woman? Is she beloved of thee?   60
I heareth ye kisseth her on the lips? Bring forth Mary of
Magdala. There shalt be on this day a royal wedding. Hurrah! Hurrah! Sendeth the heralds to trumpet the news of
the marriage of the King of the Jews. Marry her and maketh her thy queen. I shalt giveth thee my kingdom. Let   65
her giveth thee many sons to render unto David an heir to
his house! Nay, faith. I grow weary of this game. Convey
the King of the Jews back to Pontius Pilate. What sort of
sport is he? Fie! on thee. Fie!

[Friday Morning: The Palace of Pontius Pilate]
Re-enter JESUS
PONTIUS PILATE

Ye hath brought this man unto me, as one that perverteth   70
the people and behold, I, having examined him before you,
have found no fault in this man, touching those things
whereof ye accuse him: No, nor yet Herod, for I sent you
to him; and no, nothing worthy of death is done unto him.
I will therefore chastise him, and release him.   75

Luke 23:21

Luke: 23:22

belie: slander, tell lies about
decry: to speak disparagingly of; denounce as faulty or worthless
descry: reveal, disclose, make known

Luke 23:22

deify: to make a god of; exalt to the rank of a deity; personify as a deity

Luke 23:22

chastise: punish
scourge: to whip

Matthew 8:5-13

Saul *amidst the Multitudes*
    His blasphemy, the Word justifies him!
    He the Messiah is not. Deny him!
    The False Prophet standeth ye not by him.
A few of the Multitudes
    We deny him O Lord. Crucify him.
    We standeth not by him. Crucify him!   80
Pontius Pilate
    Why, what evil hath he done?
Saul
    Speaking our truths, we cannot belie[†] him!
    He the Messiah is not. Decry[†] him.
    Of his evils, ye must ye descry[†] him!
More of the Multitudes
    We decry him O Lord. Crucify him.   85
    Descry him. Yea faith! Crucify him!
Ponitus Pilate
    I canst not find any crime against him.
Saul
    The murderous Apostles ally him!
    He the Messiah is not. Defy him.
    Taketh ye pains ye not deify[†] him!   90
Many more of the Multitudes
    We defy him O Lord. Crucify him!
    Deify him. Nay faith. Crucify him!
Pontius Pilate
    I have found no cause of death in him: I will therefore
    chastise[†] him, and let him go. Taketh this "king" and ha-
    veth him thus scourged[†].   95
Centurion *witnesses to Pontius Pilate*
    Prefect, mayest I offer testimony. Whenst Jesus was en-

Isaiah 53:1-12

tered into Capernaum, there came unto him, I, a centurion, beseeching him, And saying, Lord, my servant lieth
at home sick of the palsy, grievously tormented. And Jesus
saith unto him, I will come and heal him. I answered and   100
said, Lord, I am not worthy that thou shouldest come under my roof: but speak the word only, and my servant shall
be healed. For I am a man under authority, having soldiers
under me: and I say to this man, Go, and he goeth; and to
another, Come, and he cometh; and to my servant, Do this,   105
and he doeth it. When Jesus heard it, he marvelled, and
said to them that followed, Verily I say unto you, I have
not found so great faith, no, not in Israel. And I say unto
you, That many shall come from the east and west, and
shall sit down with Abraham, and Isaac, and Jacob, in the   110
kingdom of heaven. But the children of the kingdom shall
be cast out into outer darkness: there shall be weeping and
gnashing of teeth. And Jesus said unto me, Go thy way;
and as thou hast believed, so be it done unto thee. And my
servant was healed in the selfsame hour. Punish this man   115
not, my liege.

PONTIUS PILATE

Scourge the King of the Jews. Purge me of his subjects.

The guards bind JESUS to the post in the nearby Pretorium. MARY,
MOTHER OF JESUS laments.

MARY, MOTHER OF JESUS

Isaiah, giveth comfort unto this lamented woman.
To whom thee of the arm of the LORD revealed.
For he shall grow up before him as a tender plant,   120
And as a root out of a dry ground:
He hath no form nor comeliness;
And when we shall see him,
There is no beauty that we should desire him.

The Roman Mongrel counts the number of lashes Jesus is scourged from one (1) to forty (40) in Latin. Mary speaks, the mongrels scourge Jesus, and the number of the lash is pronounced.

MARY, MOTHER OF JESUS   ROMAN MONGREL *counting lashes*

He is despised and rejected of men;	*Unus*	125
A man of sorrows, and acquainted with grief:	*Duo*	
And we hid as it were our faces from him;	*Tres*	
He was despised, and we esteemed him not.	*Quattuor*	
Surely he hath borne our griefs,	*Quinque*	
And carried our sorrows:	*Sex*	130
Yet we did esteem him stricken,	*Septem*	
Smitten of God, and afflicted.	*Octo*	
But he was wounded for our transgressions,	*Novem*	
He was bruised for our iniquities:	*Decem*	
The chastisement of our peace was upon him;	*Undecim*	
And with his stripes we are healed.	*Duodecim*	135
All we like sheep have gone astray;	*Tredecim*	
We have turned every one to his own way;		
And the LORD hath laid on him		
The iniquity of us all.	*Quattuordecim*	
He was oppressed, and he was afflicted,	*Quindecim*	140
Yet he opened not his mouth:	*Sedecim*	
He is brought as a lamb to the slaughter,	*Septendecim*	
And as a sheep before her shearers is dumb,	*Duodevignti*	
So he openeth not his mouth.	*Undevignti*	
He was taken from prison and from judgment:	*Viginti*	145
And who shall declare his generation?	*Unus et viginti*	
For he was cut off out of the land of the living:	*Duo et viginti*	
For the transgression of my people was he stricken.	*Tres et vigninti*	
And he made his grave with the wicked,		
And with the rich in his death;	*Quattuor et viginti*	150
Because he had done no violence,	*Quinque et viginti*	
Neither was any deceit in his mouth.	*Sex et viginti*	
Yet it pleased the LORD to bruise him;	*Septem et viginti*	

Deuteronomy 25:3

Mark 15:17

Mark 15:18
Mark 15:19

John 19:4

He hath put him to grief: *Duodetriginta*

When thou shalt make his soul an offering for sin,   *Undetriginta*   155

He shall see his seed, he shall prolong his days,   *Triginta*

And the pleasure of the LORD

Shall prosper in his hand.   *Unus et Trignita*

He shall see of the travail of his soul,   *Duo et Trignita*

And shall be satisfied by his knowledge shall   160

My righteous servant justify many;   *Tres et Trignita*

For he shall bear their iniquities.   *Quattuor et Trignita*

Therefore will I divide him

A portion with the great,   *Quinque et Trignita*

And he shall divide the spoil with the strong; *Sex et Trignita*   165

Because he hath poured out his soul unto death: *Septem et Trignita*

And he was numbered with the transgressors; *Deuodequadraginta*

And he bare the sin of many,   *Undequadraginta*

And made intercession for the transgressors. *Quadraginta*

SAUL

Forty stripes ye gaveth. Doth not exceed: 170

If ye shouldst exceed and beat him, I plead!

My brothers should seem lewd unto the Lord.

The ROMAN MONGRELS cease their scourging.

The ROMAN MONGRELS clothe Jesus in purple and plat a crown
of thorns, put it about his head.

ROMAN MONGRELS

Hail! King of the Jews!

They smote him on the head with a reed, and did spit on Him, and
bowing their knees, worshipped Him. Then let Him back to the court-
yard of Pontius Pilate.

PONTIUS PILATE

Behold, I bringeth Him forth to you, that ye may know

that I find no fault in Him.   175

Definition	Scripture Reference
	John 19:5
	John 19:5-6
	John 19:7
	John 19:9
	John 19:10
	John 19:11
	John 18:39
	John 18:40
	John 19:9

Then came Jeusu forth, wearing the crown of thorn, and the purple
robes.

Pontius Pilate *continuing*

> Behold the man! Take ye him, and crucify him: for I find
> no fault in him.

Saul

> We have a law, by our law, die he ought.
> Because he made himself the son of God!

Pontius Pilate

> Whence art thou?   180

JESUS is silent.

Pontius Pilate *continuing*

> Speakest thou not unto me? knowest thou not that I have
> power to crucify thee, and have power to release thee?

Jesus

> **Thou couldest have no power, at all, against.**
> **Whosoe'er deliver me hath the Sin.**

Pontius Pilate

> My custom during this feast of thine, I am wont to re-   185
> lease unto the people a prisoner whom they would. I hath
> a prisoner herewith who leadeth insurrection, is a dema-
> gogue and a thief and a murderer. Whom wilt ye that I
> release unto you? Barabbas whom is a confessed murderer
> or Jesus which is called the Christ? Whether of the twain   190
> will ye that I release unto you?

Multitudes

> Barabbas. Barabbas. Barabbas. Barabbas.

Pontius Pilate

> What shalt I do then with Jesus which is called Christ?

Saul

> His blasphemy, the Word justifies him!

John 19:15

John 19:15

Matthew 27:24

Matthew 27:25

He the Messiah is not. Defy him.   195
The False Prophet, standeth ye not by him.
Speaking our truths, we cannot belie him!
He the Messiah is not. Decry him.

ALL OF THE MULTITUDES
We deny him O Lord. Crucify him.
We standeth not by him. Crucify him!   200
We decry him O Lord. Crucify him.

PONTIUS PILATE
Shall I crucify your King?

SAUL
We hath no king but Caesar!

PONTIUS PILATE
I am innocent of the blood of this just person: see ye to it!

SAUL *continues his rabble-rousing*
Of his evils, ye must ye descry him!   205
The murderous Apostles ally him!
He the Messiah is not. Deny him!
Taketh ye pains ye not deify him!

ALL OF THE MULTITUDES
Descry him. Yea faith! Crucify him!
We defy him O Lord. Crucify him!   210
Deify him. Nay faith. Crucify him!

CAIAPHAS *lamenting*
His blood be on us, and on our children.   212

Exeunt

Definition   Scripture Reference

The Stations of the Cross by St. Francis of Assisi

A&tus Quartus - Scena Prima

[Friday: The Via Dolorosa (Stations of the Cross)]

The Women

    O most merciful Jesus,
    With a contrite heart and penitent spirit,
    I bow down in profound humility before Thy divine majesty.
    I adore Thee as my supreme Lord and Master;
    I believe in Thee, I hope in Thee,   5
    I love Thee above all things.
    I am heartily sorry for having offended Thee,
    My Supreme and Only God.
    I resolve to amend my life,
    And although I am unworthy to obtain mercy,   10
    Yet the sight of Thy holy cross, on which Thou wilst die,
    Inspires me with hope and consolation.

I will, therefore, meditate on Thy sufferings,
And visit the stations of Thy Passion
In company with Thy sorrowful Mother   15
And my holy guardian angel,
With the intention of promoting
Thy honor and saving my soul.
I desire to gain all the indulgences
Granted for this holy exercise for myself   20
And for the Poor Souls in Purgatory.
O merciful Redeemer, who has said,
And I, if I be lifted from earth,
Will draw all things to Myself,"
Draw my heart and my love to Thee,   25
That I may perform this devotion as perfectly as possible,'
And that I may live and die in union with Thee. Amen.

I. Jesus is Condemned to Death

We adore Thee, O! Christ and we praise Thee.
Because by Thy holy Cross, Thou redeems the world.

MARY MAGDALENE

Jesus, most innocent, who neither has nor could commit sin,   30
     Is condemned to death, and moreover,
     To the most ignominious death of the cross.
     The remain a friend of Caesar, Pilate delivers
     Him into the hands of His enemies.
     A fearful crime-to-condemn Innocence to death   35
     And to offend God in order not to displease men!

THE WOMEN

O! innocent Jesus, having sinned, I am guilty of eternal death,
     But thou hath accepted the unjust sentence of death,
     That I might live. For whom, then shalt I henceforth live,

Definition   *Scripture Reference*

If not for Thee my Lord? Should I desire to please men,   40
I could not be Thy servant. Let me, therefore,
Rather displease men and all the world.
Than not please, Thee, O! Jesus.

II. Jesus is Made to Carry His Cross

MARY MAGDALENE

When our divine Savior beheld the cross,
  He most willingly stretches out   45
  His bleeding arms, lovingly Embraces it,
  And tenderly kisses it,
  And places it on His bruised shoulders,
  He, although almost exhausted, joyfully carries it.

THE WOMEN

O! my Jesus, I cannot be Thy friend and follower,   50
  If I refuse to carry the cross. O! dearly beloved cross!
  I embrace thee, I kiss thee,
  I joyfully accept thee from the hands of my God.
  Far be it from me to glory in anything,
  Save in the cross of my Lord and Redeemer.   55
  By it the world shall be crucified to me
  And I to the world, that I may be Thine forever.

III. Jesus Fall For The First Time

MARY MAGDALENE

Our dear Savior, carries the cross,
  Is so weakened by its leaden weight
  As to fall exhausted to the ground.   60
  Our sins and misdeeds are the heavy burden
  Which oppresses Him; the cross is to Him
  Light and sweet, but our sins are galling and insupportable.

Definition   *Scripture Reference*

THE WOMEN

O! my Jesus, Thou shalt bare my burden
    And the leaden weight of my sins.   65
    Should I, then, not bear in union with Thee,
    My easy burden of suffering
    And accept the sweet yoke of Thy commandments?
    I therefore willingly accept it.
    I will take up my cross and follow Thee.   70

IV. JESUS MEETS HIS SORROWFUL MOTHER

MARY MAGDALENE

How painful and how sad it must be for Mary,
    The sorrowful Mother, to behold her beloved Son,
    Laden with the burden of the cross!
    What unspeakable pangs her most tender heart experience!?
    How earnestly doth she desire to die in place of Jesus,   75
    Or at least with Him! Implore this sorrowful Mother
    That she assists you in the hour of your death.

THE WOMEN

O Jesus, O Mary, I am the cause of the great
    And manifold pains which pierce your loving hearts!
    O! that also my heart would feel   80
    And experience at least some of your sufferings!
    O Mother of Sorrows, let me participate
    In the sufferings which thou
    And Thy Son endure for me,
    And let me experience thy sorrow, that afflicts thee,   85
    I may enjoy thy assistance in the hour of my death.

Definition   *Scripture Reference*

V. Simone of Cyrene Helps Jesus With His Cross

Mary Magdalene

> Simon of Cyrene is compelled to help Jesus
>> Carry His own cross, and Jesus accepts his assistance.
>> How willingly would He also permit you to carry the cross:
>> He calls, but you hear Him not;   90
>> He invites you, but you decline.
>> What a reproach, to bear the cross reluctantly!

The Women

> O Jesus! Whosoever does not take up his cross
>> And follow Thee, is not worthy of Thee.
>> Behold, I join Thee in the Way of Thy Cross;   95
>> I will be Thy assistant, following Thy bloody footsteps,
>> That I may come to Thee in eternal life.

VI. Veronica Wipes the Face of Jesus

Mary Magdalene

> Veronica, impelled by devotion and compassion,
>> Presents her veil to Jesus to wipe His disfigured face.
>> And Jesus imprints on it His holy countenance: 100
>> A great recompense for so small a service.
>> What return to you make to your Savior
>> For His great and manifold benefits?

The Women

> Most merciful Jesus! What return shall I make
>> For all the benefits Thou hast bestowed upon me?   105
>> Behold I consecrate myself entirely to Thy service.
>> I offer and consecrate to Thee my heart:
>> Imprint on it Thy sacred image,
>> Never again to be effaced by sin.

Definition   *Scripture Reference*

VII. Jesus Falls A Second Time

Mary Magdalene

The suffering Jesus, under the weight of His cross,   110
    Again falls to the ground; but the cruel executioners
    Wilt not permit Him to rest a moment.
    Pushing and striking Him, they urge Him onward.
    It is the frequent repetition
    Of our sins which oppress Jesus.   115
    Witnessing this, how can I continue to sin?

The Women

O Jesus, Son of David, have mercy on me!
    Offer me Thy helping hand, and aid me,
    That I may not fall again into my former sins.
    From this very moment, I will earnestly strive to reform: 120
    Nevermore will I sin! Thou, O sole support of the weak,
    By Thy grace, without which I can do nothing,
    Strengthen me to carry out faithfully this my resolution.

VII. The Women of Jerusalem Weep Over Jesus

Mary Magdalene

These devoted women, moved by compassion,
    Weep over the suffering Savior.   125
    But He turns to them, saying:
    Weep not for Me, Who am innocent,
    But weep for yourselves and for your children.
    Weep thou also, for there is nothing more
    Pleasing to Our Lord and nothing more profitable for thyself, 130
    Than tears shed from contrition for thy sins.

The Women

O Jesus, Who shall give to my eyes a torrent of tears,
    That day and night I may weep for my sins?

I beseech Thee, through Thy bitter and bloody tears,
To move my heart by Thy divine grace,   135
So that from my eyes tears may flow abundantly,
And that I may weep all my days over
Thy sufferings, and still more over their cause, my sins.

IX. Jesus Falls For The Third Time

MARY MAGDALENE

Jesus, arrives exhausted at the foot of Calvary,
Falls for the third time to the ground.   140
His love for us, however, is not diminished,
Not extinguished. What a fearfully oppressive
Burden our sins must be to cause Jesus to fall so often!
Had He, however, not taken them upon Himself,
They would have plunged us into the abyss of Hell.   145

THE WOMEN

Most merciful Jesus, I return Thee infinite thanks
For not permitting me to continue in sin and to fall,
As I have so often deserved, into the depths of Hell.
Enkindle in me an earnest desire of amendment;
Let me never again relapse, but vouchsafe me   150
The grace to persevere in penance to the end of my life.

X. Jesus Is Stripped of His Garments

MARY MAGDALENE

When Our Savior arrives on Calvary,
He is cruelly despoiled of His garments.
How painful this must is
Because they adhered to His wounded and torn body,   155
And with them parts of His bloody skin are removed!
All the wounds of Jesus are renewed.

consupiscence: lust, sexual desire

Jesus is despoiled of His garments
That He might die possessed of nothing;
How happy will I also die after laying aside   160
My former self with all evil desires and sinful inclinations!

THE WOMEN

Induce me, O Jesus, to lay aside my former self
And to be renewed according to Thy will and desire.
I will not spare myself, however painful
This should be for me: despoiled of things temporal,   165
Of my own will, I desire to die,
In order to live for Thee forever.

XI. JESUS IS NAILED TO THE CROSS

MARY MAGDALENE

Jesus, being stripped of His garments,
Is violently thrown upon the cross
And His hands and feet nailed thereto.   170
In such excruciating pains He remains silent,
Because it pleased His heavenly Father.
He suffers patiently, because He suffered for me.
How do I act in sufferings and in troubles?
How fretful and impatient, how full of complaints I am!   175

THE WOMEN

O Jesus, gracious Lamb of God,
I renounce forever my impatience.
Crucify, O Lord, my flesh and its concupiscence[†];
Scourge, scathe, and punish me in this world,
Do but spare me in the next. I commit my destiny to Thee, 180
Resigning myself to Thy holy will:
May it be done in all things!

Matthew 27:34-37

Matthew 27:40-43

XII. Jesus Is Raised Upon the Cross and Dies

Mary Magdalene

> Behold Jesus crucified! Behold His wounds,
>> Received for love of you!
>> His whole appearance betokens love: 185
>> His head is bent to kiss you;
>> His arms are extended to embrace you;
>> His Heart is open to receive you.
>> O superabundance of love, Jesus, the Son of God,
>> Dies upon the cross, that man may live   190
>> And be delivered from everlasting death!

The Women

> O most amiable Jesus! Who will grant me
>> That I may die for Thee!
>> I will at least endeavor to die to the world.
>> How must I regard the world and its vanities,   195
>> When I behold Thee hanging on the cross,
>> Covered with wounds? O Jesus, receive me into
>> Thy wounded Heart: I belong entirely to Thee;
>> For Thee alone do I desire to live and to die.

The ROMAN MONGRELS gave Him sour wine mingled with gall to drink. But when he had tasted it. He would not drink. They divided His garments, casting lots, that it might be fulfilled which was spoken by the prophet. Sitting down, they kept watch over Him there. And thy put up over His head the accustion written against Him. THIS IS JESUS THE KING OF THE JEWS.

Saul

> Thou! Thou that destroyest the temple and buildest it in   200
> three days, save thyself! If thou be the Son of God, come
> down from the cross. he saved others; himself he cannot
> save. If he be the King of Israel, let him now descend from

Luke 23:34

Luke 23:39

Luke 23:40-41

Luke 23-43
John 19:25

John 19:26
John 19:27
John 19:27

Elio, Elio, lama sabachthani!: "My God,   *Mark 15:34*
My God, why hast thou forsaken me?"   *John 19:28*
                                                          Matthew 27: 47,49

John 19:28
John 19:30

John 19:30
Luke 23:46

the cross and we will see and believe him. He trusted God; let him deliver him now, if he will have him: for he said, I   205 am the Son of God!

JESUS

Father, forgive them for they know not what they doest.

BAD THIEF

If thou be the Christ, save thyself and us.

GOOD THIEF

Dost not thou fear God? Speak! and ye confess! We hath committeth sins justly indeed; We receiveth due reward of our deeds.   210 But this man hath done not-a-thing amiss.

JESUS

To day shalt thou with me in paradise.

Now there stood by the cross of Jesus His mother, and His mother's sister, Mary the wife of Clopas, and Mary Magdalene. When Jesus therefore saw his mother, and the disciple standing by, whom He loved, He saith unto His mother.

Woman, behold thy son.

Then saith He to His disciple.

Behold, thy mother.

Elio, Elio, lama sabachthani†!   215

SAUL

This man calleth for Elias. Let be, let us see whether Elias will come to save him.

JESUS

I thirst.

They filled a spunge with vinegar, and put it upon hyssop, and put it to his mouth.

It is finished.

Father, into thy hands I commend my spirit.   220

Definition   *Scripture Reference*

                                                    John 19:30

                                                    Mark 15:39

And it was about the sixth hour and there was darkness over all the earth until the ninth hour. And the sun was darkened and the veil of the temple was rent in the midst. And having said thus, he bowed his head and gave up the ghost.

CENTURION

Verily, the Son of God is this man!

XII. JESUS IS TAKEN FROM THE CROSS AND
Given to His Mother

MARY MAGDALENE

Jesus did not descend from the cross

But remained on it until He died.

And when taken down from it,

He in death as in life, rests on   225

The bosom of His divine Mother.

Persevere in your resolutions of reform

And do not part from the cross;

He who persevereth to the end shall be saved.

Consider, moreover, how pure the heart   230

Should be that receives the body and blood

Of Christ in the Adorable Sacrament of the Altar.

THE WOMEN

O Lord Jesus, Thy lifeless body, mangled and lacerated,

Found a worthy resting-place

On the bosom of Thy virgin Mother.   235

Have I not often compelled Thee to dwell in my heart,

Full of sin and impurity as it was?

Create in me a new heart, that I may worthily receive

Thy most sacred body in Holy Communion,

And that Thou mayest remain in me   240

And I in Thee for all eternity.   241

Exeunt

Scena Secunda

[Friday Evening: The Tomb of Joseph of Arimathea]

XIV. Jesus Is Laid in the Sepulcher

MARY MAGDALENE

The body of Jesus is interred in a stranger's sepulcher.
>He who in this world had not whereupon
>To rest His head, would not even have a grave of His own,
>Because He was not from this world.
>You, who are so attached to the world, 5
>Henceforth despise it, that you may not perish with it.

THE WOMEN

O Jesus, Thou hast set me apart from the world;
>What, then, shall I seek therein?
>Thou hast created me for Heaven;
>What, then, have I to do with the world? 10
>Depart from me, deceitful world, with thy vanities!

Definition   *Scripture Reference*

Psalm 30:1-12

Henceforth i will follow the Way of the Cross
Traced out for me by my Redeemer,
And journey onward to my heavenly home,
There to dwell forever and ever.   15

Exit MARY MAGDALENE, the WOMEN, and the MEN car-
rying JESUS.

The stone is rolled over.

VOICE OF JESUS

I will extol thee, O Lord; for thou hast lifted me up,
And hast not made my foes to rejoice over me.
O Lord my God, I cried unto thee, and thou hast healed me.
O Lord, thou hast brought up my soul from the grave:
Thou hast kept me alive, that I should not go down to the pit. 20
Sing unto the Lord, O ye saints of his,
And give thanks at the remembrance of his holiness.
For his anger endureth but a moment; in his favour is life:
Weeping may endure for a night, but joy cometh in the morning.
And in my prosperity I said, I shall never be moved.   25
Lord, by thy favour thou hast made my mountain to stand strong:
Thou didst hide thy face, and I was troubled.
I cried to thee, O Lord; and unto the Lord I made supplication.
What profit is there in my blood, when I go down to the pit?
Shall the dust praise thee? shall it declare thy truth?   30
Hear, O Lord, and have mercy upon me:
Lord, be thou my helper.
Thou hast turned for me my mourning into dancing:
Thou hast put off my sackcloth, and girded me with gladness;
To the end that my glory may sing praise to thee, and not be silent. 35
O Lord my God, I will give thanks unto thee for ever.   36

The body of Jesus disappears from within the burial shroud, which col-
lapses as the stone rolls away.

Exuent

Mark 16:3

Mark 16:6

Aɛtus Quintus - Scena Prima
[Sunday Morning: Outside the Tomb]

Enter MARY MAGDALENE and the OTHER MARY.

Mary Magdalene
　　Who shall roll away the stone from the door
　　Of the sepulcher? Wherein art our Lord?

A YOUNG MAN sits on the right side, clothed in a long white garment.

Young Man
　　Be not affrighted. Ye seek the Nazarene.
　　Look ye about the tomb. Is he not seen?
　　Fear not ye: He who suffered crucifixion　　　　　5
　　Is not here. Ye seek He who is risen.
　　Come women, see the place where the Lord lay.
　　He who is risen goest into Galilee.
　　Let his disciples know, quickly goest.

Definition	*Scripture Reference*
	John 20:13
	John 20:13
	John 20:16
Rabboni: teacher	*John 20:16*
	John 20:17
	Luke 24:17
	Luke 24:18
	Luke 24:19
	Luke 24:19

Seek ye the living. Seek ye ne'er a ghost.   10
JESUS

Woman, why weepest thou? Whom seekest thou?
MARY MAGDALENE

Sir, if thou have borne him hence, hear my vow.
Gardener, who hath this tomb invaded?
I wilt taketh Him where thou hast laid him.
JESUS

Mary.   15
MARY MAGDALENE

Rabboni†!
JESUS

Toucheth me not; to my Father ascended
Am I not yet. But go to My brethren.
Say unto them. My Father am I brought.
My Father, your Father, my God, your God.   20

Exit Mary Magdalene

[Sunday Morning: The Walk to Emmaus]
JESUS

What manner of communications hath
Ye unto one another, and are sad?
CLEOPAS

Art thou to Jerusalem a stranger?
Hath thou not known the things that come to pass?
JESUS

What things?
CLEOPAS

What things? He who wast born of a manger;   25
Mighty in deed and Word of God wast harassed
By the chief priests condemned Him to the cross

gecks: fools

Psalm 38:19

(Fullfilled Matthew 27:14) Zechariah 13:7

(Fulfilled Matthew 27:9-10) Zechariah 11:12

espereance: hope, expectation, optimism
disease: grief, sin   *(Fulfilled Matthew 8:16-17) Isaiah 53:4*

raft: a great quantity; a lot   *(Fulfilled John 1:29) Isaiah 53:5*

chastisement: punishment

Isaiah 53:6
(Fullfilled John 19:1)
(Fulfilled Matthew 27:14) Isaiah 53:7

And wouldst have left Him in the mud like dross.
A kind friend, secret disciple, from whom
Offered our Lord burial in his tomb.   30
Three days hath been since these things accomplished.
Yea! and certain women were astonished
When they found not His body, came and spake
To His disciples that the earth doth quake.
Our Rock found it as the women hath said;   35
Romans stealeth our Lord, filleth us dread.

JESUS

O! gecks†, slow of heart to believe the Word;
Ought not the Christ for thy sins hath suffered
And to enter into glory, ne'er more to dread?   40
Prick thine ears, hearken what the prophets said:
David King spake, His enemies art strong.
Their hate is multiplied fore'er, yet wrong.
Zechariah sayeth, Smite the Shepherd
And all of his sheep to the wind scattered.   45
Giveth Judas a price, if not forbear,
Weighed price of a score and ten of silver.
And shalt they look upon me whom was pierced
And shalt they mourn their espereance† most fierced.
Isaiah spake, He hath borne their disease†,   50
Their sorrows carried for their esteem.
Smitted of God and mortification:
Wounded was I for thine raft† trangressions.
Bruised was I for thine iniquities,
Chastisement† of peace for thine penalties.   55
All ye sheep hath gone astray from thy pens,
Howbeit my pain with these stripes art thy cleansed?
Oppressed was I and afflicted was I,

(Fullfilled Matthew 13:14-15) Isaiah 6:9

(Fullfilled Matthew 27:35) Isaiah 53:12
(Fullfilled Matthew 27:34) Psalm 69:21
(Fulfilled Mark 16:6) Psalm 16:10

(Fulfilled John 19:33-36) Psalm 34:20
(Fulfilled Matthew 27:46) Psalm 22:1
(Fulfilled Luke 24:51) Psalm 68:18

e'ening: evening   *Luke 24:29*

Luke 24:30

Luke 24:31

Luke 24:32

Not my mouth open, not escape a cry,
The smoking flax ne'er was quenched. In the street   60
Ne'er heard my voice, nor broke the bruised reed.
Was I brought as a sheep before the butcher.
As a sheep is dumb before her shearer.
Israel heard me, yet they believed not.
And they didst see me, yea, but perceived not.   65
Was not I numbered with the criminals?
Didst I drink vinegar mixed with some gall?
Wilt my soul suffer fore'er behind Hell's gate?
Neither wilt I suffer corruption's weight.
Yet keepeth all my bones from being broken.   70
My God, My God, why was I forsaken?
To holdeth all captivity captive;
To ascend on high so that ye may live.

CLEOPAS

For it is towards e'ening†, with us abide.

CLEOPAS, *his friend, and JESUS sit.*

Here is bread to eat, and wine to imbibe.   75

JESUS

Take, eat: this is my body
Which is broken for you.
This do in remembrance of me.
Take, drink: this is my blood
The blood of a New Covenant   80
Which is shed for you.
This do in remembrance of me.

JESUS *vanishes out of their sight.*

CLEOPAS

Whence He spake, did not our heart within burn?
Whilest He talked with us by the way of scripture.

Definition	Scripture Reference
	Luke 24:36
	Luke 24:38-39
	John 20:25
print: hole, impression	*John 20:25*
	John 20:27
	Matthew 28:19
	Luke 24:44-46

[Later: Hiding Place of the Disciples]

JESUS

    Peace be 'to you, from My Father I goest.   85

    From Me you goest. Receive ye the Ghost.

    Whoe'er soe'er sins ye remit, remitted.

    Whoe'er soe'er sins ye retain, retained.

    Why are ye troubled; why heart's fear rise?

    Behold my hands and my feet, them handle.   90

    For a spirit no flesh and bones disguised.

    Hath ye here any meat to 'void scandal?

Enter THOMAS

PETER

    Thomas! Thomas! We hath seen us the Lord.

THOMAS *not seeing the Lord*

    Except shalt I see his hands, print[†] of nails

    And putteth my finger in the print of nails.   95

    And thrusteth my hand into his side.

    I wilt not believe. Thy lies ne'er I abide.

JESUS

    Reach hither thy finger, behold my hands.

    Thrust in' my side, hither reach thy hand.

    Thomas, thou hast seen me, thou hast believed.   100

    Bless'd art they that have not seen, yet believe!

Gathering the DISCIPLES together

    Go ye into all the world o'er the earth

    And preacheth the gospel of e'ery creature.

    Baptize he that believeth in the Lamb;

    But he that believeth not shalt be damned.   105

    What I speakest, whilst I was with ye still.

    The Law of Moses, Prophets, Psalms fulfilled.

    The Prophets spake. The Prophets hath written

Luke 24:50-53

Hebrew Psalms

Jewish Publication Society (JPS), a translation of the *Hebrew Bible* published in 1917

Glossary Bibliography

David Crystal and Ben Crystal 2002. *Shakespeare's Words: A Glossary & Language Companion* New York: *Penguin Books*
dictionary.reference.com

Thus it behoved the Christ to be smitten.
On the third day, repentance! Remission   110
Of sins! preach to nations! Jerusalem!   111

And he led them out as far as to Bethany, and he lifted up His hands, and blessed them. And it came to pass, while he blessed them, he was parted from them, and carried into heaven. And they worshipped him, and returned to Jerusalem with great joy and were continually in the temple praising and blessing God. Amen!

Fin.

Scenario #1

The Greatest Story
as it has never been told before.

by William Ireland

The second decade of the 17th Century saw the creations of the greatest dramatic works by the poet, playwright, actor, and theatrical entrepreneur, William Shakespeare and the greatest prose ever composed in the English language, the King James "Authorized" Version of *The Holy Bible*.

To many Christians, the works of William Shakespeare are crude and lewd, full of debased debauchery. To many Roman Catholics, the King James *Bible* smacked of sacrilege and heresy. Shakespeare was denounced on the pulpit and King James was decried by the Papacy. Strange bedfellows indeed.

Strangely, the Bard never wrote a play concerning the life of Jesus the Christ, whose Gospel many English people were only now discovering the story of in their native tongue, a living language. Until this point in our history, the Roman Mass was spoken and sung entirely in a dead language: Latin.

Why was William Shakespeare silent concerning the Greatest Story Ever Told? While not the most adept writer of original plots, Shakespeare had adapted many stories that were completely unknown to English audiences, because they originated in other European languages. But here was the Gospel being printed and preached to the our people in our own language by our popular King, yet the Bard, a popular playwright, chose not to write a play about, the most bestselling book ever printed in English.

There have been rumors for years that William Shakespeare, the most prized of English poets, was enlisted by the Translators of the King James "Authorized" Version to translate many of King David's Psalms into English.

Conspiracies that swirl around pubs and university libraries speak of William Shakespeare, in his forty-sixth year, riddling the forty-sixth Psalm by translating the forty-sixth word from beginning of the Psalm as "shake" and the forty-sixth word from the end as "spear". Coincidence? More than likely not. (Sorry to disappoint, Mr. Anthony Burgess, but this theory is quaint, *Ed.*)

While labouring as a Translator to the "Authorized" *Holy Bible*, Shakespeare would have had incredible access to the original Greek and Hebrew texts as well as the ear of many fine Translators. Would he have passed on the opportunity to write a play concerning the most dramatic and world-altering week in the life of the Son of the Living God, Jesus the Christ?

There is a proposition that perhaps he did. He wrote the most *Divine Tragedy of Jesus the Christ* for performance at the Globe during 1611. Would the censors, the esteemed men of high morals who considered theater as a lewd and crude artform, deem the *Divine Tragedy* as not fit for the eyes of the people of court, city, or country. Did the very thought of a lowly actor, Richard

Burbadge, putting on the mask of the Lord and Saviour Jesus the Christ strike the Crown as blasphemy? Could such a play be fit for performance?

I fear the swift stroke of the censor's quill signed the death warrant to what may have proved to be Shakespeare's greatest work. A notice nailed to the door to the Globe would have announced to playwright, actors, and passing populous that this play would be barred from production. The King's servants, no doubt, collected all of the "foul papers", the play scripts and the promptbooks. Being damned as heresies against the Church, they would be burned, like human heretics, not at the stake, but upon the pyre. An ironic fate, indeed.

With no proof of the *Divine Tragedy of Jesus the Christ*, the magnificent play fell from living memory and died the most horrendous of literary deaths: forgotten for time immemorial.

Or did it?

affect: to desire earnestly; seek after

bewitched: stolen

acceptation: kind reception, a receiving with favour or approbation

baggage: offense

pit: poor people paid a penny to stand in the area in front of the stage.

Richard Burbadge: actor who played Hamelt, Lear, Othello,

confounded: ruined

children: words born of his mind

exercised: made familiar

bowel: compassionate feelings

laud: a song of praise

confusion: shame

banished: censored

Eloi, Eloid, lama sabachtani: "My God, My God, why hast thou forsaken me?"

Sonnet 155
by William Shakespeare

O! Kinge, how canst I, of the pen, affect'd[†]?
Thy thief of language hath bewitched[†] my words
Thy acceptation[†] of my script reject'd!
How canst the Gospel in the church be heard?
My words art of Heaven, nary of Hell,
I implore thee tell me of God's baggage[†]
Howbeit the pit[†] art deaf to my Gospel!
That the Christ canst not be played by Burbadge[†]?
Confounded[†] are my children[†] exercised.
My bowels [†]of praise, Halleluah! I laud[†]!
To common man of Jesus crucified!
Confusion[†] for staging the Word of God?
    Banished[†] my words by thy royal decree,
      "Eloi, Eloi, lama sabachthani?"[†]

Definition

Robert Barker: the printer of the King James Version of the Bible
starker: complete
Vicar: Pope
gawking: staring
tome: book
sooth: truth
tongue: language
obseisance: bowing, obedience
confound: shame
admiration: wonder
dewing: painting, writing
gleens: glisten
palmerworms: an destructive caterpiller; bookworm.
digest: destroy, distort
living language: English (Latin being considered a "dead lanuage")

Sonnet 156

Stood I at the shoppe of Robert Barker[†]
The might of English scripture shown.
The light of the Gospel was most starker.[†]
The Vicar [†]crieth from Peter's High throne.
Stood I at the shoppe gawking[†] at thy tome[†]:
Howbeit by thy decree, an English Gospel!
Howbeit the sooth[†] of Christ so far from Rome?
Canst by the English tongue[†] in churches tell.
Thy neck's obseisance[†] the Pope's guillotine
To confound[†] the Pope; the admiration[†]
For dewing[†] the Gospel, in English gleens[†]
The Gospel of Christ in our mother tongue!
    Catholic palmerworms[†] diges[†]t the Word.
    In a living language[†] must be it heard!

Melpomene: Greek Muse of tragedies
two score: forty
Heraculean task: Heracles was given 12 impossible task.
Globe: the name of Shakespeare's theater.
distort: adapt
fitted: approved by the authorities
scourge: whip
pleasures: entertainment
pit: poor people paid a penny to stand in the area in front of the stage.

Sonnet 157

O Muse! Melpomene[†]! Thy tragic mask.
I, for two score[†] days and for two score nights,
Doth labour on theHeraculean task[†]
To bringeth to the Globe[†] the light of Christ.
To distort[†] Holy prose to poetry
Fit[†] for the stage. Neigh! for on the pulpit
The priests scourge[†] with barbed words they on their knees.
Is Latin tailored to the Gospel fit?
For the pleasures[†] of the pit[†], doth I stage
The Passion of Jesus Christ for their eyes.
I pray, God! the Vicar doth cry in rage.
The Words of Christ in English? O! despise!
    Doth the"Gospel According to Shakespeare"
    Of the fires of the pyre to burn must fear?

Scenario #2

What is in a name?

by Orson Welles

"I am... haunted by the conviction that the divine William is the biggest and most successful fraud ever practiced on a patient world."

Henry James

"It is my final belief that the Shakespearean plays were written by another hand than Shaksper's [sic]... I do not seem to have any patience with the Shaksper argument: it is all gone for me- up the spout. The Shaksper case is about closed."

Walt Witman

ORSON WELLES: What's in a name? That which we call Shakespeare- by any other name would smell just as sweet? I think Oxford wrote Shakespeare. If you don't agree, there are some awfully funny coincidences to explain away... I'm not alone in my feelings. Freud was adamant about it. Olivier and Gielgud, arguably the greatest Shakespearian actors of my generation, believed as I do. Mark Twain, for criminy sakes wrote a book about it! Emerson? Whitman! How could you possibly not?

PETER BOGDANOVICH: Your argument is that Edward de Vere took the *nom-de-plum* William Shakespeare and presented plays as such? Why? Is it because as a member of the aristocracy, an Earl of Oxford couldn't been seen writing something as common as plays?

OW: *Nom-de-plum?* Heavens, no. I'm not suggesting anything of the sort. Not a "pen-name". Mercy. Not even a pseudonym. An allonym. This is a completely different literary creature all together. A wicked little fraud and deceit utilized by many of the greatest philosophers, wordsmiths, statesmen, and, yes, apostles. This is what allonymous is all about.

PB: I'm not quite sure I know what "allonymous" is?

OW: A pseudonym is writing under a fictional name not your own and anonymous is writing under no name. Allonymous writing is writing under an actual historical person's name.

PB: Why would anyone want to publish under someone else's name? Isn't that akin to plagiarism?

OW: Heavens, no. It's the exact opposite of plagiarism. Plagiarism is taking someone else's words and claiming they are your own. Allonymous is taking *your* words and claiming they are *someone else's* words. They can't be any more different.

PB: Then it's more akin to forgery.

OW: Forgery? Again, you can't be more wrong. Forgery is taking, say, the Mona Lisa and painting another Mona Lisa and passing yours off as the original Mona Lisa. Allonymous is painting something new and exciting and saying, "Look! This could be an entirely new Leonardo DaVinci. Prove me wrong."

PB: Then in my opinion, it's worse than plagiarism and forgery.

OW: Oh, ye of little faith! It is grand and glorious. And it is far more common than one would think. After Plato's death, his students continued writing philosophical tracts in his name. No one in their time or for hundreds, nay, thousands of years, thought this was in any way deceitful. They were carrying on Plato's own tradition by continuing his thought... in his name. This is writing allonymously. Alexander Hamilton, one of the founding fathers of our country, wrote with a couple of compatriots, the *Federalist Papers* under the name of the Roman official Publius. This gave the *Papers* and, ultimately the young nation, an air of historicity it desperately needed. Are these great men frauds and their words fraudulent?

PB: I'm not quite sure, given your argument.

OW: Was William Ireland a forger for publishing *Vortigern and Rowena* and *William the Conqueror* as authentic Shakespeare? If Shakespeare didn't actually write Shakespeare, how can we fault Ireland for writing "Shakespeare"? There were many plays written during Shakespeare's own lifetime that people of his day thought were actually written by Shakespeare. There was no doubt whatsoever in the minds of audiences and critics that these suspect plays were written by William Shakespeare. These plays are now considered "apocryphal" because scholars say they may not have been actually written by the pen of William Shakespeare of Stratford-upon-Avon. Ironically, there is some scholarly movement lately concerning *Two Noble Kinsmen* and *Edward III*, which says that these two once apocryphal plays are actually part of the legitimate Shakespearean canon. Hilarious. Who is to say, who wrote what? Scholars? Bah. Did Moses write the Torah or was it some Hebrew priest hundreds of years after the fact? Did

Matthew write *Gospel of Matthew*? Or Luke *Luke*? Many scholars… hmmph… think a disciple of Paul actually wrote at least one of the letters attributed to Paul. Is the Word of God any less the word of God because of the writer? Is Shakespeare any less Shakespearean if written by Edward de Vere? The words are the words are the words.

PB: I can see your point.

OW: The point is, I don't even know the point I was trying to make. Some people have a stick up their butt about authenticity. Is Hamlet any less magnificent if written by the Earl? Or a woman as some others suppose. Scholars claim that if Shakespeare didn't write Shakespeare than all is for naught. The plays are brilliant no matter their authorship. Shakespeare or de Vere? Apocryphal or canon? It does not matter. I have a little story to tell.

PB: Do tell.

OW: An antique bookstore owner came to me, of all people, to look at a copy of an early 17th Century quarto a collector claimed was play called *The Gospel According To Shakespeare* by William Shakespeare. Now, this wasn't the title of the play itself. The play was called *The Divine Tragedy of Jesus the Christ*, but the play was subtitled by the publisher of the quarto, *The Gospel According to Shakespeare*. To my untrained eye, it was authentic. I don't think it was an actual 17th century manuscript. That I know for sure. It may have been a later reprint of an earlier manuscript, I don't know. It seemed to be derived from foul papers, this I knew.

PB: Foul papers?

OW: Shakespeare, or de Vere, never published his own plays. They were published by others from different types of play scripts. Some were promptbooks given to actors, but this proved hinky because most promptbooks cut many of the other actors' lines out of other actor's copies. The actor had their lines and their cues and that was it. The publisher needed several copies of promptbooks to reconstruct a complete play. Others scripts were foul papers, or rough drafts by the playwright that may not have the revisions made during and after production included in them. All this made getting a complete version of any Shakespearean plays difficult during the first few folios. *The Gospel According to Shakespeare* appeared to be foul papers because it looked to have been drawn from a rough draft of a Shakespearean play, perhaps from early in the rehearsal period. The author may have been pressured by time to finish the play for its benefactor. I can imagine old Edward huddled around a candle in the cold of the London winter trying to get the play finished in time for Lent. He was just running out of time. Turn all of the parables into iambic pentameter? That'll take too long. They're stories. Just keep them in prose. Prose isn't bad. Falstaff, the greatest character in Shakespeare never spoke in poetry. There were other apparent short-cuts made indicating it was, in fact, foul papers. The stage directions, for instance, were taken practically verbatim from the King James version, as if the author just threw up his hands to the actors and said, "Just do what the Bible says you're supposed to do." Hell, that sounds like it would be spoken from the pulpit not the prompt.

PB: At what point in your career did this rare-book collector come to you?

OW: A little after my *Macbeth* was a success. My name was wagging on everybody's tongue. This was the first time in my career that would happen. The first, but unfortunately, not the last.

PB: Ah, the voodoo *Macbeth*.

OW: Oh, how a loathe that phrase. *Voodoo* MacBeth! Well, yes. It was shortly after I was Broadway's darling and only a few short years before I became Hollywood's pariah. As a lover of everything Shakespeare, it had always struck me as odd that Shakespeare never tackled the life of Christ. If there is no other life in all of history that was more important to have written a play about, I'm at a loss for what it could be. The Passion of Jesus written in iambic pentameter! A passion play by the hand that wrote *Hamlet*! Imagine. Why in the hell didn't Shakespeare or de Vere or whoever, write the Passion of Jesus? If I hadn't held that quarto in my greedy little hands, I would have wanted to write a Shakespearean passion play myself and publish it allonymously as William Shakespeare.

PB: What if you did actually did write it? It would prove within your character.

OW: Touché. But I'm not sure I'd have the mettle to tackle meter in such an undertaking. Transposing *Macbeth* to Haiti is one thing, scaring the entire nation with a radio drama is a second thing, but writing a new Shakespeare play in iambic pentameter and passing it off as authentic is another thing entirely. No one in nearly 400 years has written a play in Shakespearean-style verse. There has to be a reason for this. It simply may not be possible given the evolution of the English language. For a Jacobean Englishman to write iambic Jacobean English in pentameter, is certainly one great accomplishment. But for a playwright in the intervening centuries? Impossible. What if what I wrote was bad Shakespeare? I don't think my psyche could handle the criticism. Whose could? I tell you, I think counterfeiters and forgers have the hardest art.

PB: Art? Don't you mean crime?

OW: No. Of course, it's an art. You spend your entire careers perfecting your craft to impossible standards, mastering mimicry, and you can't even take credit for your work. You don't put your own name on it. You put someone else's name on it. Allonymously! We've come full circle. If you're great, nobody will ever be the wiser. If you're terrible, you're exposed as a fraud and hoaxer and damned to the ninth circle of Hell with all of the other traitors. Ah, for the anonymity of the forger. I could write iambic pentameter if I had the desire, but it would be bad Shakespeare.

PB: And what if it was great Shakespeare?

OW: I'd have to take immediate credit for the actual authorship. Whoever wrote *The Gospel According to Shakespeare* should have taken credit for it. I know I would have. I would have stood on that stage in front of my full house and said, "Shakespeare? Bah. The Bard was a hack. He ran a proverbial iambic gin mill churning out masterpieces of the English language. *I* wrote the Passion of Jesus in *Shakespearean* verse! *He* never tackled the subject. *He* was probably scared to tears to write something as epic as the Passion of Jesus the Christ! It wasn't even that hard. I wrote it in what? Twenty-six days. Hell, forget Shakespeare. Praise me! I am the rightful heir to the legacy of Shakespeare!" But I didn't write it. Allonymously or not. How I wished it was authentic. From the pen of Shakespeare-upon-Avon or the Earl of Oxford, I could care less. It was such a fascinating and superb play. I should have produced it right then and there, while I was still on Broadway.

PB: If only you had known then what you later discovered with the *War of the Worlds* radio broadcast, just how effective a little slight-of-hand is in the marketing and promotion of a production, a staging of *The Gospel According to Shakespeare* would have been a gold mine. A long lost play by William Shakespeare, can you imagine? Even as a forgery, it would have played for years.

OW: But I didn't know then what I know now. I don't even know now what I knew then! I wouldn't have had the career I had if I had known what I know whenever I knew it.

PB: Wow, my head is spinning.

OW: Your head? My mouth. But I never saw them again; the quarto and the rare book dealer vanished like a fart in a whirlwind. I wondered in the years since if that wasn't a ghostly apparition of the Bard himself manifesting itself, desiring some belated recognition for their passionate work on the Passion of Jesus.

PB: What impressions did you get from the play. Could it have been authentic? Or was it a masterful forgery?

OW: From what I remember, it was a little short for a Shakespearean play and obviously obsessed with rhyming couplets. This marked the play as early in Shakespeare's career, but the King James Version of the *Holy Bible* wasn't published until 1611, very late in his career.

PB: But if Shakespeare didn't write Shakespeare?

OW: Oh, ye of great faith. I will play the Devil's Advocate against myself. Given that ol' Oxford died seven years before King James published his "authorized" version of the Bible, how can this Shakespearean play be written by a dead man before the source material was even published? It still makes no matter; Oxford, no doubt, had a copy of Tyndale's *Holy Bible*, which His Majesty authoritatively plagiarized throughout the KJV. So this passion play could have been written early in the career of said playwright, Shakespeare or de Vere, take your pick, or it could have been written late in their career and perhaps even after their own death, which de Vere would have had to have accomplished given a few glaring timeline difficulties. Every play from *Timon of Athens* and on would have had to be been written before de Vere died in 1604 and produced patiently and posthumously at regular intervals for nearly a decade. Holy hell, I'm blowing holes in my own theories here. Stop me, Peter, before I go any further.

Scenario #3

H for Hoax

by Clifford Irving

Hoaxery (not exactly a word, but are we splitting hairs over faking a word?) requires intuitive forethought with a premeditated and conscious effort to deceive. Not the least of which require the skills of:

- CONFIDENCE MAN: The art of the "long con", as grifters like to call it, begins long before the mark ever meets him and essentially and effectively ends the moment the mark truly believes that the idea is actually theirs. The hoaxer knows intuitively that he will be believed because of (not in spite of) the believability and/or ridiculousness of his idea.

- MASTER FORGER AND COUNTERFEITER: The forger and counterfeiter agonize over the slightest imperfection of the color or texture of the paper, the chemicals used to age and otherwise affect the paper, and every stroke of their pen or engraving in their silver plate. Likewise, the hoaxer obsesses over every minute detail of his hoax, attempting as best he can to foresee every possible challenge to his hoax and have an appropriate rebuttal.

• Fortune Teller: The hoaxer, not unlike a fortune teller, feeds off of the eagerness of their victims to believe and provides them with the precise story they are most willing to accept as true.

• Parlor Magician: Both the parlor magician and hoaxer use misdirection to make their audience believe they have seen what they haven't actually seen and will have claim to have seen until their dying day.

• Stage Actor: The stage actor uses suspension of disbelief- the audiences' willingness to lay aside their logic and rational intellect to believe every word occurring on a stage only a few feet away.

• Career Politician: And finally, but certainly not least, just as a career politician spends a lifetime pandering to his constituency, the hoaxer gives his marks everything they are looking for and more, leaving them, the majority of the time, satisfied and completely unaware they were duped.

Hoaxes, as a matter of definition, also require a victim, known to the above professions by such colorful and poetic names such as mark, dupe, or pigeon. Each victim has certain personality traits that "mark" him as a "pigeon"; which are known to include an over eagerness to believe, being easily susceptible to suggestion, a willingness to suspend their disbelief, or an innate need to trust.

* * *

Literary hoaxes have a long and storied history. My own, *The Autobiography of Howard Hughes*, is still whispered about in literary circles and is hailed as the supreme example of a hoax that was nearly successful due to the subject's obsessive reclusiveness. I had almost pulled it off. Other literary hoaxes are successful because the "author" is dead; many years, decades, or if the hoaxer has chooses his subject well, centuries dead. This may have been my downfall. How was I supposed to know that a notorious recluse who had not spoken in public for decades would denounce me so publicly?

The Hitler Diaries were a contemporary of my *Autobiography* and both were ridiculed as obvious forgeries. This point I take offense to. Konrad Kuto, a hackneyed forger from Stuttgart, made little to no attempts to forge anything."With the exception of imitating Hitler's habit of slanting his writing diagonally as he wrote across the page," Kenneth W. Rendell noted, "the forger failed to observe or to imitate the most fundamental characteristics of his handwriting."

Where is the art of the forgery? I slaved over that copy of *Newsweek* magazine, sweating blood over every subtle penstroke. Because of, not in spite of, my choosing a contemporary celebrity figure, I didn't have to stalk antique book stores, like a tomb robber, looking for blank leaves from historical manuscripts from the era of my hoax, nor did I have to manufacture inks with the same chemical signatures as inks used during said time-period. All I needed was a pen, some fine stationary, and a great deal of artistic and literary skill to perpetrate my hoax.

The publisher and editor of *The Gospel According to Shakespeare* confessed to me, in their letter, that this is a modern work by a 21st Century poet, but they wanted a hoaxer's opinion of its "hoaxery" (this word again, but theirs not mine). Their questions and concerns are:

- Is *The Gospel According to Shakespeare* effective enough in its style and meter to succeed as a hoax?
- If so, should the play be published as an authentic work of William Shakespeare?
- What are the legal and moral consequences of hoaxery, fraud and forgery?
- Is it worth the consequences to publish this book?

I fear they prefer to hide behind the term "allonymous" which they consider to be their second best option in publishing this play. "Allonymous" is a word I thought they made up, until I looked it up in an older and admittedly heftier dictionary from my library. Now that I understand the historicity of "allonymous" works. It fits entirely into their marketing. It is certainly the safer road. This I know all too well.

They will not claim that this is an "authentic" Shakespearean play, which is their right, but this is cowardly. They should have the will to proclaim to the world that they have discovered a long lost play written by William Shakespeare and not only that, it is a passion play about the last week of Jesus Christ's life.

If the works of William Shakespeare were indeed written by the Seventeenth Earl of Oxford-Edward de Vere, Francis Bacon the statesmen and poet, or by playwright Christopher Marlowe, then the works were actually written allonymously. William Shakespeare was a contemporary of both, who is known to have worked in the theater as a lowly actor and minor theatrical entrepreneur. But the claim that there little to no proof he had the education nor the literary talent to write the plays attributed to him. If de Vere, Bacon, or Marlowe had actually written *Hamlet*,

Julius Caesar, or *Henry the V*, they published their plays, not under the pseudonym "William Shakespeare", but the allonym "William Shakespeare". It is splitting literary hairs, but entirely plausible. I am an indentured Stratfordian; Shakespeare wrote Shakespeare. There is no doubt in my mind about that.

But in the realm of hoaxery, it is an exquisite story. I didn't write allonymously. I had the courage to put my own name on the cover of my *Autobiography of Howard Hughes*. I didn't hide behind the literary hokum of allonyminity. As if this absolves the author, editor, and publisher from the charges of forgery. When caught, I accepted by fate and spent my time in prison. They want the notoriety of a great forgery, but don't want to suffer the legal consequences. Cowards.

As to the "hoaxery", it fails on a few counts, but succeeds on many more. The poet's mimicry of Jacobean English is exemplary, but given that the King James version of the Bible, which is the primary source, was also written in Jacobean English, this is not as impressive. The poet, ignoring the modern impression that poetry should not rhyme, is overly concerned with rhyming couplets. However, the beauty of his poetry is extraordinary and the consistent rhyming and meter does force the author into phenomenal and inconceivable word choices.

I am not expert enough in poetry to determine if the lines of dialogue are written in iambic pentameter. I am not about it sit here with a dictionary and go over every single word in this play to determine where the stressed and unstressed syllables are. I counted the syllables in each line and there are ten in each and almost every line. This is close enough to iambic pentameter for me.

The play does use a few sources that William Shakespeare could not possibly have had access to. *The Gospel of Thomas* was discovered near Nag Hammadi, Egypt, in 1945 and the *Gospel of*

Judas, the primary source of Judas' strange and heretical soliloquy in the second scene of act two, was not made public until October 2006. A hoaxer should never use a source that wasn't available to the subject of the hoax.

I know an author would say the Shakespeare had access to sources to his own canonical plays that he should not have possibly had access to due to chronological discrepancies or language barriers. The ancient Church Fathers had mentioned these particular texts in the first few centuries of the common era, so there could have been a theological awareness of them in the early 17th Century. But William Shakespeare possessing these texts is stretching the matter too much for this master of hoaxery.

I will say, "Bravo!" to the author for having the audacity to write a new play in Shakespearean verse. It has been what, nearly 400 years, since someone had the courage to write a play in iambic pentameter? I chose the most famous and infamous subject in Howard Hughes for my *Autobiography*, so I commend the author for choosing the passion of Jesus as the subject for his Shakespearean play. I am impressed that any modern poet would tackle both the subject and style with such authenticity and bravado. This is both bold and audacious. Whoever he is, he is a master mimic. Bravo!

In the end, I, Clifford Irving, declined their invitation to write an introduction for their impressive, but ultimately little book. I told them, if they are so bold, they can write their own damn introduction and put my name on it: allonymously. Let's see if they have the *cojones*.

Scenario #3½

Confessional

by Robert Dwight Brown

"Father, forgive me, for I have sinned..."

And it came to pass that a poet and playwright, in the second decade of the 21st Century, was inspired by the tragic Muse Melpomene to sit at his computer, stare blankly at an empty Word file for a bit, crack open an edition of the King James Version of *The Holy Bible*, and listen to the distant and indistinct voice of William Shakespeare. The Bard called out to me across the centuries to write what he failed to write: a play in Shakespearean verse concerning the Passion of our Lord and Saviour Jesus the Christ.

Over twenty-three sleepless days and twenty-three inspired nights, I wrote the *Gospel According to Shakespeare*. Here I present it to you, as I wrote it. The spirit of Shakespeare, my mentor and muse, haunted me as a schizophrenic hallucination. Through these inspired words, I wish to inspire you with the faith of the Word of God, written in Shakespearean verse. May the light of Christ shine bright on stage or on film through the *Gospel According to Shakespeare.*

May the grace of our Lord Jesus Christ be with you all. Amen.

Notes for Directors

I.

Sources

The King James "Authorized" Translation of *The Holy Bible* is the primary source for the play. The pseudenomical texts of *The Gospel of Thomas* and *The Infancy Gospel of Thomas* were used for the testimonies of the false witnesses against Jesus during His trial before the Sanhedrin.

The *Gospel of Judas*, as translated from the Coptic original by Rodolph Kasser, Marvin Meyer, and Gregor Wurst, in collaboration with Francois Gaudard and published by National Geographic, was bastardized in Act 2i as a soliloquy uttered by Judas.

In Act 4i and 4ii, the Stations of the Cross were written by St. Francis of Assisi and are included in the *Gospel According to Shakespeare* practically verbatim. The prayers are given to the women in Jesus' life: his mother Mary, Mary Magdalene, Martha and her sister Mary, amongst others. The action of these Stations play out as they are described in the medieval text. The Gospels are strangely silent pertaining to these events.

* * *

II.

Including Saul of Tarsus

The inclusion of Saul of Tarsus in a Passion Play is controversial to say the least. Many Christians are convinced that Saul/Paul never met Jesus while He walked the earth prior to His crucifixion, even though the Bible is silent on this point.

Saul was present at the stoning of Stephen the first martyr in Jerusalem (*Acts* 7:54-60), circa 34 A.D. If Saul had been an instigator in the great persecution against the church which was at Jerusalem (*Acts* 8:2), then it is not only possible but extremely likely that Saul, a Pharisee who was son of a Pharisee, would have been active in the Sanhedrin, present in Jerusalem for Passover in 30 A.D., and the Pharisee who persecutest Jesus (*Acts* 9:4) in that mockery of a trial.

III.

Authorized Edits

There are two soliloquies in *The Gospel According to Shakespeare* that may prove to be too controversial for Christian audiences, particularly productions held inside churches. Herod's entire crude, cruel, and blasphemous speech can be cut from Act 3i along with Pontius Pilate's preceding "Sayeth thou Galiliee?..." dialogue. The scene would jump from Saul's line to Pontius Pilate's dialogue immediately after Herod's soliloquy.

Judas' long soliloquy in Act 2i may be too strange and heretical for Christian audiences and can be substituted with the following:

JUDAS

> Jesus is a false prophet! He's no Christ!
> From the shadows, thy debate I hath heard;
> The while my fellow disciples slumber.

Nay, faith. A betrayer of God, I ne'er.
My belief in Jesus hath been an err.
A maid, with some spikenard, a precious oil,
Anointed his head, like Samuel 'to Saul,
Crowning him "King of the Jews". Jesus spoils
To waste nine and six score pence, O! the gall!
He heal'd the blind with paste from whence he spat.
He is not of God, he keeps not the Sabbath!
He curseth a fig tree in his hateful strife!
For the tree of the field is but man's life!

IV.

The Crowds

MULTITUDES, PHARISEES, SADDUCEES, DISCIPLES, MONEY CHANGERS, DOVE PEDDLERS, SINFUL SHEPHERDS, CHILDREN'S CHORUS, and ROMAN MONGRELS are considered "crowds". Their dialogue is not intended to be spoken by just one member of the crowd, but by many of the crowd. How this works for your particular production is up to you. You many have specific lines read as a "chorus" (i.e. by many voices at once) and/or you may divide specific lines up amongst many different members of the crowd, including many smaller choruses as well. This gives the director freedom to make these dialogue passages have as an epic feel as possible with large or small casts.

www.ingramcontent.com/pod-product-compliance
Lightning Source LLC
LaVergne TN
LVHW011348080426
835511LV00005B/185